MW01632081

KAVANAGH
Q.C.

KAVANAGH Q.C.

STARRING

JOHN THAW

The official story behind the hugely popular ITV drama

GEOFF TIBBALLS

CARLTON

THIS IS A CARLTON BOOK

This edition published by Carlton Books 1996

ISBN 0 7475 2517 X

Executive Editor: Lorraine Dickey
Art Direction: Zoë Maggs
Project Editor: Nicky Hodge, Nigel Matheson, Sarah Larter
Production: Sarah Schuman

Main front cover photograph by Terry O'Neill/Carlton UK Television shows John Thaw as James Kavanagh Q.C. Back cover photographs by Tony Nutley/Carlton UK Television. Top left shows Lisa Harrow as Lizzie Kavanagh, Nicholas Jones as Jeremy Aldermarten and John Thaw as James Kavanagh Q.C. Photograph, middle right, shows Anna Chancellor as Julia Piper. Photograph, middle left, shows John Thaw as James Kavanagh Q.C., Daisy Bates as Kate Kavanagh, Tom Brodie as Matt Kavanagh and Lisa Harrow as Lizzie Kavanagh.

Printed and bound in Great Britain by
Butler & Tanner Ltd, Frome and London

Contents

INTRODUCTION

The making of Kavanagh Q.C.

A year ago, a new name, James Kavanagh, joined the ranks of British television barristers, a tradition which dates back to Michael Denison as the elegant Boyd QC in the Fifties and blossomed through the inimitable Rumpole of the Bailey. The new series, *Kavanagh Q.C.*, stars one of our most popular and versatile actors, John Thaw, as a man who has climbed to the very top of his profession...sometimes at the expense of his home life.

Extensively researched and with superb production values, *Kavanagh Q.C.* was immediately judged a hit by viewers and critics alike and was praised for its dramatic storylines and compelling authenticity. It wasn't long before a second series was commissioned.

This book goes behind the scenes of the programme, revealing why the barristers' wigs are dipped in coffee, why the costume designer once went shopping for swastikas and why John Thaw initially turned down the role.

Kavanagh Q.C. has been hailed as the most accurate legal series to date. Within these pages, you will find the reasons why.

I rest my case.

Geoff Tibballs

JOHN THAW AS JAMES KAVANAGH Q.C.

Chapter One

Preparing the brief

Ted Childs and John Thaw go back a long way. In the mid-Seventies, Childs was producer of The Sweeney, *the series which first made John Thaw a household name.*

Nine years after Regan and Carter screeched off into the sunset, it was Ted Childs who commissioned the hugely successful *Inspector Morse* series. John Thaw took the title role as the enigmatic detective who sought to stem the ever-rising body count in once tranquil Oxford. But all good things come to an end and once the Morse series reached its natural conclusion – only resurrected for the occasional one-off film – Ted Childs, as managing director of Central Films, set about looking for a new vehicle for Thaw.

'Although he agreed to do the odd Morse, I think John had probably had enough of playing policemen,' says Ted, 'and in any case I wanted to do something different. It seemed to me that a liberal lawyer, one concentrating mainly on defence, would be an interesting idea. So I put it to John.

"Will I be on a hot set all day wearing a wig?"

'The plan was to shoot it in summer. John said: "Will I be on a hot set all day wearing a wig?" It so happened that I'd just read an article in the paper which said that our barristers would soon be copying the American mode, so I stated with some confidence: "No, they'll soon be doing away with all that." As it's turned out, the wigs are still with us, so poor John has had to spend two summers, the last one exceptionally hot, on set all day in wig and gown.'

John Thaw recalls: 'Ted came up with the idea of me playing a barrister when we were doing Morse and knew it was coming to an end as a series. I remember saying no because I didn't want to wear a silly wig, but Ted said, by the time we began making it, they would have got rid of wigs. They actually had a vote but the anti-wiggers were outvoted! But by then Ted had twisted my arm and anyway I was hooked on Russell Lewis' script.'

Chris Kelly (producer of the first two series of *Soldier, Soldier*, as well as being a novelist, scriptwriter, broadcaster and presenter of *Food and Drink*) was brought in to produce the new series. He says: 'Another writer had come up with elements of the show, including a couple of the character names, but Ted and I felt that the script didn't really work. So we got Russell Lewis, for whom I have enormous admiration, to write the first one.

'Ted, John, Gina Cronk (then Head of Drama Development) and I developed the character of Kavanagh together. One of the first problems to be solved from my point of view was how to distance John Thaw from Morse – a character with which he had been synonymous over a number of years – without being too contrived, like giving him a red nose and a pair of horns! By coincidence, before Kavanagh began I'd been hired by LWT to write two scripts about pupil barristers. It is ironic that the idea eventually fell through because Kavanagh had come along. But while researching that project over a period of three or four months, I had met a lot of legal people and that stood me in good stead for Kavanagh. I mixed with them, sat in the clerks' room and listened to the way they talked. I spoke to pupils and a lot of young female barristers who told me some extraordinary stories. I went to various types of court to try and get as broad a picture as I could. Not only that, but my brother Bernard is a QC and, although he didn't practise as a barrister – he's now chairman of an industrial tribunal – it gave me a grounding in that world.

'From what I saw and heard, my concern was that the whole world of the law was too middle-class, and so it was desirable, both in terms of the show's appeal and in terms of dramatic interest, to make Kavanagh from the other side of the tracks. That's why we gave him working-class roots.'

LIFE HAS NOT ALWAYS BEEN THIS HAPPY FOR KAVANAGH AND HIS WIFE LIZZIE.

The working-class-boy-made-good angle also helped distance Kavanagh from Morse, as did the presence of a wife, Lizzie, and two teenage children, Kate and Matt – a total contrast to Morse, the archetypal loner. A third key difference was Kavanagh's hair! Chris reveals: 'As part of our research, John and I went to watch Michael Mansfield QC in the

Royal Courts of Justice, and it was seeing his long, flowing grey locks that gave us the idea for Kavanagh's hair. It was all part of our process of making him distinct from Morse.

'Like many people, I was brought up on the Rumpole view of the law which was hugely enjoyable and successful, but not intended to reflect reality. Rumpole was a great character but the truth is he wouldn't last three days in chambers now. The pace of life is much faster these days. Anyway, I wanted to do something different, to set Kavanagh in the real world.'

"...Ted worked through from A to Z. Eventually he alighted on 'Kavanagh' which sounded just right"

Russell Lewis is one of our foremost television writers. He specialises in crime series, his credits including *The Bill*, *Between the Lines*, *Taggart*, *Cadfael* and *Wycliffe*, and so he was the natural choice to pen the all-important opening episode of *Kavanagh Q.C.*

'Actually,' says Russell, 'the central character was called Lawton at first. I remember Ted Childs, Chris Kelly, Gina Cronk and myself throwing names around. None of us could come up with a name we were really happy with, and so Ted worked through from A to Z. Eventually he alighted on 'Kavanagh' which sounded just right. The K and the V gave it an impressive feel, together with a hint of Irish. And so Kavanagh it was.

'What we didn't want was "Morse dons a wig" so we gave him a family, and I deliberately set the opening case in his native Manchester. He defended a boxer on a charge of GBH – so that we could include that family background. We had his mum and dad in court while his brother and sister-in-law came along for lunch afterwards. We also wanted to give our hero problems at home – we weren't looking for a happy family man. The aim

THE MODEL PROFESSIONAL – KAVANAGH OUTSIDE HIS CHAMBERS.

was to show him to have a very different vulnerability to Morse.

'For the same reason, we didn't want to feature a murder case in the opening episode. It would have had too many echoes of *Inspector Morse*. So I came up with a rape case. I consulted various books about rape and discovered that not that many rapes which come to trial bring a guilty verdict. I was also keen on exploring miscarriages of justice – but where someone was wrongfully acquitted instead of wrongly convicted. So I gave it that twist at the end where the student was acquitted but it then emerged that it was highly probable that he had been guilty all along.'

JOHN THAW DISCUSSES A TECHNICAL POINT WHILE FILMING AT PORTSMOUTH FOR THE EPISODE 'THE BURNING DECK'.

Audience research had also revealed that viewers particularly like a twist at the end of an episode.

'We've been extremely lucky to have a real barrister, David Bradly, as our legal adviser,' says Russell Lewis. 'He's been a great help to all the writers. I recall a Sunday morning spent in his chambers just listening to him talk. From that came the form of Kavanagh's courtroom speeches. In fact, it was David who suggested Kavanagh's plan of attack in Episode One. And he's never afraid to pick you up on things. I wrote one speech for a judge which I quite liked – it was pure Rumpole – but David said things like that just don't happen.

'I've done a fair bit of research, attending trials, although my own personal court experience is confined to two sessions of jury service. I remember one was a heavy drugs case and the jury, despite overwhelming evidence, voted 10-2 to return a not guilty verdict. I was one of the two! I was astonished at how little the evidence seemed to matter to jurors – it was much more a question of whether or not they liked the look of somebody. The other thing which struck me was the diplomacy and politeness between counsel and the bench. Everyone knows what they really mean but it's all couched in such polite terms.

'I enjoyed developing the other characters too. We didn't want to lumber Kavanagh with being Head of Chambers, so we gave that to Peter Foxcott. And Jeremy Aldermarten represents everyone's idea of what a barrister is. He is a rather sad, lonely figure who leads an exotic fantasy life. I wrote a scene in which fellow barrister, Julia Piper, whom Aldermarten has a crush on, talked about life at an all girls' school. It really got Aldermarten going.'

The idea for Kavanagh was first mooted in August 1993 and Russell Lewis remembers putting the finishing touches to the draft script on New Year's Eve – to the despair of his wife – for submission to the ITV Network Centre. In January 1994, *Kavanagh Q.C.* was given the go-ahead by the ITV chiefs. 'We were one of five legal series up for consideration,' says Chris Kelly, 'but ours was the one they felt most positive about. I think having John Thaw might have helped too...'

NICHOLAS JONES WAS A UNANIMOUS CHOICE TO PLAY BARRISTER JEREMY ALDERMARTEN.

With John Thaw already in place, Chris Kelly, Colin Gregg (the director of the first story) and casting director Joyce Gallie set about selecting the rest of the regular cast.

'I really enjoy casting,' enthuses Chris, 'and we all tend to agree on the right person. It's not always anything to do with their CV, it's a gut instinct in the end. When they shut the door to leave the room, usually all three of you say, "Yes!" You instantly know. For instance, with Nicholas Jones and Aldermarten, we felt that no one else in the world could play that character. It was the same with Oliver Ford Davies as Foxcott. And we were thrilled to get a leading actress like Lisa Harrow to play Kavanagh's wife, Lizzie. Because we've got such a strong principal cast, it's easy to get good guest stars – people like Geraldine James, Alison Steadman, Michael Williams and John Wells.'

Joyce Gallie agrees. 'Actors think it's a quality series, so they're happy to be associated with it. Of our regular cast, obviously Lisa Harrow was a real coup for us. And Anna Chancellor was always my first choice to play Julia. I've known Anna since she left drama school and, from the moment I saw the first script, I knew that she would be ideal for the part. She brings so much to the role – she's very witty, unusual, Kay Kendallish. And it was a lucky break for us when she was catapulted to stardom by *Four Weddings And A Funeral*.

'We saw quite a few people for Aldermarten – I'd seen Nicholas Jones in the play *The Deep Blue Sea* and he was wonderfully pompous in that, yet vulnerable underneath. And those were exactly the qualities we were looking for in Aldermarten. We were also very lucky to get Oliver Ford Davies – I'd always wanted to cast him in something. We originally envisaged the senior clerk, Tom Buckley, as an older man but I adore Cliff Parisi. We knew Cliff would bring humour to the role – he's so good at playing Cockney wide boys. Considering the characters in chambers don't always get a lot to do, we really do have a wonderful supporting cast. Indeed such is their ability that I have little doubt that they could have held the series in their own right.

'We saw a lot of young actors for Kate and Matt but we achieved the right balance with Daisy Bates and Tom Brodie. They were cast separately because we weren't worried about them looking similar. Brother and sister often look completely different and, anyway, talent is more important than looks.'

“...Lisa Harrow was a real coup for us. And Anna Chancellor was always my first choice to play Julia”

Filming began in May 1994. Chris Kelly recalls: 'One of the problems we had to overcome was where to film the court scenes. We usually have to be in court for seven or eight days at a time, so we can't use ones which are in commission. And there are only a limited number of courts that are out of commission, some of which are out of London. For the first series, we shot one in Oxford and we also used the Rumpole Old Bailey set which we erected at Jacob Street Studios near Tower Bridge. We also found an old magistrates' court at Stratford East which is highly photogenic. Sometimes we shoot in real courts on a Sunday if we're only there for a short while. On other occasions, we dress buildings to look like courts. In Episode Five of this series, we've converted the interior of Chiswick Town Hall and it's worked very well.

'Our fictional River Court chambers are modelled loosely on the Queen Elizabeth Building in Middle Temple. For the first series, we built them in the old Holborn Town Hall but, by the time we came to do the second series, they were selling the building, so we built a set at our production base, an old British Telecom building in Tooting.

'The other regular location is Kavanagh's house. We felt he wasn't a man who would live in a smart Georgian terrace – we thought he'd have a bit of green around him – and

JOHN THAW JOINS THE NAVY DURING A BREAK IN FILMING AT PORTSMOUTH.

we found a place overlooking Wandsworth Common with a beautiful garden and terrace.

'We've been extremely rigorous in our research into how the legal system works – the courts, life in chambers and how barristers operate. We visited chambers at Queen Elizabeth Buildings and King's Bench Walk and talked to barristers, pupils and clerks. I found them very hardworking, very focused and extremely motivated – I particularly admired their intelligence and ability to grasp so much detail. The way they can master a brief in a very short time is amazing. I found that aspect rather alarming because they often have, for various reasons, such a short a time to get their head round a case. It's certainly not an ideal system. Sometimes barristers are handed a case just a few hours before it kicks off.

"We've been extremely rigorous in our research into how the legal system works – the courts, life in chambers and how barristers operate"

'There are certain similarities between barristers and army officers, whom I researched for *Soldier, Soldier*. The majority are from the same public school background and, like the army, there's a lot of classism and sexism.'

The four-part first series of *Kavanagh Q.C.* was transmitted in January 1995. It attracted nearly 14 million viewers and received considerable critical acclaim. In *Today*, Pam Francis wrote: 'The dialogue has been consistently sparky, the courtroom arguments compelling and the characters well drawn...If there is any justice, *Kavanagh Q.C.* will be back to fight another day.' Margaret Forwood in the *Daily Express* wrote that it was 'executed with enough panache to make it very watchable indeed'. The *Evening Standard* described it as 'a cracking series'; the *Daily Telegraph* referred to its 'glossy production values and authentic whiff of quality'; the *Times* called it 'a quality product, with strong scripts, polished photography and top-notch casting'; the *Daily Star* praised 'the tense courtroom scenes' as being 'bang on the button'; and the *Sun* hailed it as a 'Tuesday television treat'.

The only blot on the landscape came when the Independent Television Commission upheld a complaint about the rape scene in the opening episode. The commission said: 'Some explicit description of rape during court proceedings, as well as sound effects during sexual intercourse, were inappropriately scheduled during family viewing time' – before the 9pm watershed.

The ITC accepted Central's argument that the treatment of the issue was serious and responsible, but disagreed that audience expectations of frankness had changed sufficiently to permit an 8pm screening.

Writer Russell Lewis was understandably dismayed by the ruling. 'I certainly didn't set out to upset anybody and I really don't know how we could have done it any differently. It seems strange to me that you can show horrific scenes on the early evening news but, if you deal with a subject responsibly in serious drama, you get pilloried.'

With the first series proving so successful in every other way, Chris Kelly had no

KAVANAGH'S INCISIVE CROSS-EXAMINATIONS MAKE HIM A FORMIDABLE ADVERSARY IN COURT.

intention of tinkering with a winning formula. 'However for the second series I did feel we should involve Kavanagh more emotionally in stories. Obviously you can't have advocates who are bleeding hearts because, like surgeons, they can't afford to get too involved with their clients or they'd go barmy. Nevertheless, we wanted to feature stories with big emotional impact.

'From the start, we have been determined to feature a wide variety of cases for Kavanagh. It's easy to get the impression from television legal series that all criminal barristers ever do is defend murderers. Not so. Apart from anything else, they often prosecute, and so we've shown Kavanagh prosecuting as well as defending, although he tends to do more of the latter. Barristers may also be called upon to appear in a range of other sorts of hearing, both criminal and civil. For instance, George Carman, who has made a name for himself in libel cases, is sometimes hired to do cases which are quite outside his area of expertise, simply because clients believe he can bend his talents as an advocate to other briefs.

“We wanted to feature stories with big emotional impact”

'For the second series of six stories, we've been able to introduce an even greater variety. Among the cases Kavanagh takes on are drug smuggling, an industrial accident, the murder of a policewoman and a Naval court martial. The court martial story is different from anything we've done before because the whole story is told in court.'

The episode is written by Russell Lewis. He says: 'I've always wanted to do a court martial story. I'm a great fan of World War Two movies – all that British stiff upper lip. And the Navy is a great place to do it. Tradition is everywhere in the Navy and I thought it would be interesting to introduce civilians like Kavanagh in to that closed world. And I hope it will provide a window for viewers to see what takes place on these occasions, because it is something which very few will ever have experienced. Besides, the court martial happens to be a very fair and effective system.'

Chris Kelly also wanted to make sure that Kavanagh did not appear infallible in this series. 'I felt it was important that, unlike Perry Mason, Kavanagh should lose some cases. In reality, criminal barristers lose around 25 per cent of cases, and Kavanagh should be no exception. Though he shares some of the qualities of the man on the white horse, he also has his full quota of foibles. However, I don't want him losing too many, otherwise people will wonder what they're paying him for!

'We have been extremely lucky in getting such good writers on *Kavanagh QC*. Russell Lewis and Adrian Hodges, who wrote two episodes apiece in the first series, both got to grips with the legal world and did a wonderful job with the characters.

'The feedback has been good. When John Thaw was at Blenheim, near Oxford, filming an episode of *Inspector Morse* last year, an American lawyer, who had just seen Kavanagh on a transatlantic trip, told him that it was the most factual legal series he'd ever seen. So that was highly gratifying – it's always nice to know you're doing it right.'

FILMING ABOARD HMS VICTORY PROVIDES ONE OF THE HIGHLIGHTS OF THE SECOND SERIES.

VICTORY GR 1803
VICTORY GR 1803
VICTORY GR 1803
VICTORY GR 1803

CHAPTER TWO

From script to screen

Taking a television drama series like Kavanagh Q.C. *from script to screen is virtually a year-round process. Filming the second series of* Kavanagh *took place from June to December 1995 but the planning had actually started the previous January.*

JOHN THAW SHELTERS FROM THE ELEMENTS.

Producer Chris Kelly recalls: 'In January, I was looking at writers, seeing how many of the production team from the first series were still available, looking at the direction the new series would take and the way in which various characters would develop. For instance, we knew that Anna Chancellor, who plays Julia Piper, wouldn't be available to do a third series, so we had to tailor her character over the second series, so that we could say good-bye to her.

'Our legal adviser, David Bradly, is involved right from the start with discussing script ideas and he then reacts to every draft, pointing out things which may not be quite right. The trick of the series is to hold the line between what David regards as legally accurate and what we need in terms of telling the story. I like to think we're authentic in every detail although occasionally we do have to make minor amendments. In the rape story, it was pointed out that defence counsel would not have called the defendant as his last witness, as Kavanagh had done. That was an instance where we changed the sequence of evidence for dramatic effect. I felt that the end result worked better on screen than it would have done had Kavanagh called the defendant first.

'David looks through the scripts for procedural details. There's a considerable difference between the way you and I would write a court scene and the way an advocate would approach it, and it's very difficult for writers to get a grasp on the legal mind. Usually a barrister will want to elicit two or three facts from a cross-examination. One of their rules is, never ask a question you don't know the answer to. There's no waffle. They go straight for the throat. It's a question of getting that technique down on paper, of building bits of information into the

cross-examination which tell the story but which aren't repeating what has been said earlier. Then it's a matter of building to a climax.

DURING THE LONG HOT SUMMER, CAST AND CREW WERE AT THEIR HAPPIEST SHOOTING OUTSIDE.

'The best writers are also the busiest writers so you have to get them when you can, which can mean frustrating waits. And scripts don't always work out. The writer will spend around six weeks on the first draft and, since all of our scripts have produced five drafts, we're talking about a total period of something like three months per script. Obviously we work on several at once. On one recent draft alone, we spent 30 hours in meetings.

'I was looking for an additional writer for the second series and I found a pile of scripts at Central, one of which nobody had read. It was by Matthew Hall. It was about a young barrister and I thought it was a really remarkable piece of writing. What's more, it was his first effort – he had never had anything on TV. It turned out he was an ex-barrister so, hardly able to believe my luck, I commissioned him to do two scripts for the new series.'

“Usually a barrister will want to elicit two or three facts... there's no waffle, they go straight for the throat”

By February, Lars Macfarlane had been brought in to the new series as associate producer. 'At that stage,' recalls Lars, 'the plan was for four 90-minute films but the first series proved so successful that the network said it wanted six. In mid-March, we began crewing up (we were lucky to be able to get a lot of the crew from the first series) and we set up offices in Brewer Street, Soho, but we desperately needed a much larger base. Holborn Town Hall, where we'd shot our chambers scenes in the first series, was up for sale but, because we felt Kavanagh would continue to be a success, we decided to design and build our own set, so that it could be packed up at the end of the series, stored then re-erected for the next run. This, we decided, would prove economically viable if the show was going to have a long-term future.

'The set was quite expensive to build but we couldn't go into a studio because, although the barristers' chambers are featured in every episode, it is often just for two days and it is not economic to rent studio space for two days in every twenty.'

The search began for an empty office block attached to an empty warehouse. Eventually suitable premises were found – a disused British Telecom building in Tooting, south London, tucked around the back of a Gateway supermarket. The setting may have seemed unlikely but it fitted requirements perfectly.

FOXCOTT'S ROOM IS ADORNED WITH LEGAL PORTRAITS.

'10,000 square feet of silent warehousing is not easy to find,' says Lars. 'Warehousing often backs on to other warehouses where there's lots of activity. For filming purposes, we wanted somewhere quiet – we didn't want a place where trucks were going in and out all the time or which was near a railway line. And, of course, because most of our location filming is done in and around London, we needed a base that was within easy reach. In fact, the set was being built before we had even found a site, so it was a close-run thing. The set then had to be transported to Tooting, leaving production co-ordinator Liz Watkins and myself little time to set everything up before filming got underway.'

The chambers set was designed by Michael Pickwoad for whom the new location had to provide great freedom and flexibility. He explains: 'Constructing our own set means that we can put everything where we want it. For example, at Holborn, the room we used as the senior clerk's office was on the far side of the corridor. Now we've been able to move him nearer to the barristers, making the whole thing more compact and easier to operate in. Having said that, another advantage is that we have been able to make our set slightly bigger than Holborn. We've now got doors on both sides of the corridor, which we didn't have before. There are supposed to be 28 people in River Court, so when we designed the set, we put in extra doors, behind which all the barristers, whom we never see, are presumed to work. You have to be able to visualise life beyond the set. In one episode, a boy comes into chambers through a lift. We'd never had a lift before, so we had to work out which door he would be most likely to come through. The actual lift sequence was filmed somewhere else entirely.

'At the same time, we have been able to make the set more like our role model in Middle Temple. Obviously I visited chambers and studied the buildings. We have been able to blend the classical style with a mix of 17th and 18th century and to incorporate lots of traditional mud colours. I hope the end result measures up to what people imagine chambers to look like.'

Designing the set for *Kavanagh Q.C.* took Michael Pickwoad between two and three weeks. The construction team then built it in four. But it is more than just a collection of flimsy walls and hidden scaffolding. The little finishing touches in each room add that vital air of realism, even when you know that the view from Kavanagh's office window has been painted on to a backcloth.

Michael went to great lengths to ensure that the place had the right feel to it. 'Lady barristers' rooms tend to be rather overdecorated compared to those of their male counterparts, with very lush curtains, so we've made Julia's room prettier than Kavanagh's. His is much darker, to give that feel of the Garrick Club. Foxcott's room has early 18th century panelling – like hundreds of rooms in the Temple – and a lot of style. Many of the rooms have curious fireplaces, and we play around with the design to make them work on screen. There is also an abundance of legal portraits in real chambers. We usually hire these from a picture company although if we need a portrait of someone in particular, as we did in the Navy episode, we get a photo, blow it up and mount it on canvas.

“Eventually suitable premises were found – a disused British Telecom building in Tooting ... tucked around the back of a Gateway supermarket”

'For photographs on desks, you can use anyone – sometimes the actor's family – if the characters are not known. For example, photographs purporting to be of Aldermarten's aunt and uncle could be of absolutely anybody because we don't know them as characters. Obviously you have to draw the line – you couldn't use a photo of someone like Mick Jagger or Michael Jackson! And sometimes the crew will put a photograph on set and it's only afterwards that you realise it's of an actor from a previous production. That could be recognised by an eagle-eyed viewer, so you do have to be careful.

'The other thing we have on Kavanagh is paperwork – piles of it. On one case we did, the brief amounted to five piles of papers, each three inches thick. We go out of our way to ensure that the top few sheets, those that might be seen on camera, are wholly authentic in the way they look. We got hold of papers from chambers to study their layout. Prosecution papers are set out differently to those of the defence. Prosecution papers are well prepared, well organised and extremely neat, whereas the defence papers are rather more haphazard, simply because they never have the same amount of time to prepare for a case. So Kavanagh is given different papers, depending on whether he is prosecuting or defending. Similarly, when we did the Naval court martial, we were shown the proper papers that they would use so we could reproduce them accurately.

'With so much paper needed, we can't possibly type out every single sheet, so the bulk of the brief is made up of old scripts. But we do like to make the top sheets look right, even if nobody other than the actor sees them. I always think that it helps the actor to have something that appears realistic. It enables them to feel comfortable. And that is another reason that we try to make the chambers – and indeed all our sets – look authentic. It all helps with the actor's characterisation.'

As well as housing the chambers, Tooting is home to the 60-strong production team. The key moment in the production process is the delivery of the script. With the first episode in a series, the script usually arrives two or three weeks before shooting begins

EACH CASE MEANS A MOUNTAIN OF PAPERWORK FOR KAVANAGH TO WADE THROUGH.

but thereafter scripts tend to turn up progressively later, causing hair to be torn out by the handful. The designer and the director of a particular episode go through the script and decide upon the feel of the show. Then they call in the location manager and discuss where the scenes might be filmed.

FINDING THE RIGHT LOCATION IS A KEY PART OF THE PRODUCTION PROCESS.

Location manager David Kennaway says: 'I try to find buildings which can be made to look what we want or, alternatively, I try to find the real thing. If you can come up with the real thing, it's obviously better because it's cheaper and quicker since you don't have to go to the trouble of dressing it up. Once I've found a couple of likely venues, I take a few Polaroids and show them to the director. We then go out on a recce and, when the director has made his choice and we have decided exactly when we want to film, I approach the owners of the premises for permission. I find that the name of the series opens doors, so that most people are perfectly happy to let us film. And we always promise to leave a place in the same condition as we found it – sometimes better.'

Once permission is given and a financial agreement has been reached, a technical recce takes place about a week before filming. This is attended by, among others, the location manager, the director, the designer, the director of photography and the production buyer.

Each episode of *Kavanagh Q.C.* is filmed over a period of between 18 and 20 days. As associate producer, Lars Macfarlane is responsible for the day-to-day running of the operation. 'We come up with a schedule and work out a call sheet which is issued each day and is a menu for the next day's shoot. The call sheet is prepared by the second assistant director in liaison with the first assistant director whose name goes on the actual sheet. Sometimes, because of adverse weather conditions or some technical difficulty, we don't know until late on what the precise order of shooting is for the next day. The key is not to wrap at the end of the day – which is usually 7pm – without issuing a call sheet, but it has been known for call sheets to be slipped under people's hotel doors if it is really late at night.'

“An actor's life is not always pure, unbridled glamour”

The call sheet details who and what are required as well as when and where. It catalogues the scenes which are to be shot, the transport that is required and the times at which crew and cast (and by now the guest artists have been cast too) are needed on set. There is also a list of the day's prop requirements which can include such items as Kavanagh's briefs (the papers not the underwear), a football, prop drinks (invariably fake), Kavanagh's pen, a china tea set and a slop bucket. And, for good measure, the call sheet contains the all-important weather forecast. Filming usually commences at 8am which means an early start for all concerned. In order to be on set on time, allowing for prior visits to wardrobe and make-up, John Thaw has to be collected from his London home at around 6.15am. An actor's life is not always pure, unbridled glamour.

DIRECTOR OF PHOTOGRAPHY NIGEL WALTERS (LEFT) AND DIRECTOR PAUL GREENGRASS.

LINING UP SHOTS AGAINST THE BACKGROUND OF HMS VICTORY FOR 'THE BURNING DECK'.

'The trucks are on the move even earlier,' says Lars, 'often at 4am. When we're out filming, we carry with us a big road train of trucks, including mobile dressing-rooms, make-up and wardrobe caravans and catering buses. It's like a travelling circus. And the mobile loo, known as the Honeywagon, follows us everywhere. One of our biggest problems is finding somewhere to park all the trucks, particularly in Central London. That's why filming Kavanagh's house overlooking Wandsworth Common is ideal – we can park everything on the common. The courtroom scenes can be the biggest headache because they feature so many people – juries and court officials as well as the principal cast – over such a long period. On those occasions, we need more trucks than ever.

'Wherever we go, we're entirely self-sufficient. Even power and water are not essential. If need be, we can fill all the tanks up with water the night before and run the equipment on generators. We can go off to the middle of nowhere and gradually this mobile city will assemble early in the morning. The whole thing is like a military operation...and the enemy is time.'

Although the average filming day lasts ten hours (including one hour for lunch), just five minutes of what you ultimately see on screen is shot during that time. At the end of each day, the film goes to the laboratory and the rushes are processed overnight. The film is then transferred on to videotape and sent to the editors at Tooting where it is entered into a hi-tech, 'non-linear' editing machine. The two editors on Kavanagh, Dave Blackmore and Roger Wilson, edit alternate episodes.

Roger Wilson enthuses: 'The new machines we have are so much faster than the old method where you have reels and reels of tape. Each shot from a scene is represented on screen by little square tiles which are like mini photographs and can be blown up to any size you want. The other advantage is that this system allows you to keep copies of everything.

'I look through the rushes with the director and we make a few choices as to which shots are best. I then choose some sequences which I show to the director and take on board his comments. When we've been through everything and got the episode to virtually the right length, we show it to the producer, listen to whether he has any further suggestions, and then it is shown to the executive producer. It takes roughly two weeks from the end of filming the episode to come up with a fine cut.

'Once everybody is happy with the visual content, the composer, John Keane, becomes involved. The producer, the director, the composer and the editor get together to decide where the incidental music will go. From there, it's given to sound editor Simon Gershon and he and the director will suggest where any sound effects should be added. In one episode, we cut from Strasbourg, where Lizzie Kavanagh had been working, to London and we asked Simon to lay an off-screen tube train on the cut back to London because the sound of that instantly says "London". The sound track will tell you that the action has switched. It's a bit more subtle than those famous old establishing shots of Big Ben or a red London bus that used to be in Sixties film series!'

Since Kavanagh is a dialogue-led show, there isn't really the call for any unusual sound effects. The sound of a bull elephant mating, for example, is unlikely to be needed in a programme about a London barrister. 'The sound editor has CDs of various sounds,' continues Roger, 'but, if he does need something which he hasn't already got, he simply goes out and records it.

'In addition to sound effects, the director might like to add a little extra dialogue here and there if the sound's a bit flat. And often, at the end of a particularly incisive cross-examination, the natural reaction is for there to be a certain amount of muttering among the people in court. This isn't usually done when we film the courtroom scenes, so we'll need to insert that, using our own voices. I have muttered professionally! Many's the time I've had a call from Simon asking: "Will you come down for a mutter?"

'The other thing the sound editor has to do is produce a sound track for foreign language versions. This is called a music and effects track and contains no dialogue but all the sound effects, including things like footsteps and doors being opened. The countries to which Kavanagh is sold can then put their own dialogue onto the sound track.'

When the home sound track is finished, that and the visual track are sent to a theatre where the two are mixed together. Opening titles and credits are added and another episode of *Kavanagh Q.C.* is ready for its admiring audience.

DIRECTOR CHARLES BEESON (STANDING, LEFT) STUDIES A PLAYBACK.

Chapter Three

Life in chambers

There are some 7000 barristers in the City of London, each a member of one of the four Inns of Court – Lincoln's Inn, Gray's Inn, Middle Temple and Inner Temple.

A London barrister's life begins as a pupil in chambers. Pupillage usually lasts a year, divided into the 'first six' and the 'second six', during which time a pupil will be put in the charge of a junior, an established barrister. All advocates in chambers are juniors unless, and until, they 'take silk'. In the 'second six', pupils are granted rights of audience and can appear for clients, usually in magistrates' courts. Some chambers pay their pupils around £12,000 a year, while others expect them to work, and learn, for nothing. Consequently, large overdrafts are commonplace. The aim of every pupil – an ambition which, for many, becomes almost obsessive – is to gain a tenancy in chambers at the end of the pupillage year. As long as they keep their noses clean and, more importantly, keep on the right side of the senior clerk, they can then expect a job for life.

“a top criminal QC, or ‘silk’, as they are known, will probably earn between £200,000 and £300,000 a year”

Sets of chambers are not necessarily located at the Inn to which each barrister belongs. For example, Kavanagh is a member of Gray's Inn but his chambers, 5 River Court, are in Middle Temple. Each set tends to specialise in civil law, criminal law, family cases, tax matters or whatever. Oddly enough, the criminal bar is not regarded as particularly desirable. Since most criminal cases are legally aided, the financial rewards for a barrister are considerably less there than they are in, say, insurance cases. That is where the rich pickings are. Nevertheless, a top criminal QC or 'silk', as they are known, will probably earn between £200,000 and £300,000 a year.

A barrister becomes a 'silk' simply by applying to the Lord Chancellor, usually some 20 years after first being called to the Bar. If they don't succeed at first, they can try again. The period after 'taking silk' can be hazardous. Fees rise with the appointment, and the solicitors who favour the junior-turned-silk may be reluctant to pay the extra.

JULIA PIPER RELISHES ACTING AS KAVANAGH'S JUNIOR.

Each set of chambers – often housed in a building of which Dickens would have been proud – is presided over by a Head of Chambers, usually the senior 'silk'. He or she acts rather like the Master of an Oxbridge college. Various committees of barristers, dealing with anything from new computers or the selection of pupils to sanitary arrangements, report to the Head of Chambers. The Head will also play host on social occasions, such as at a party thrown to celebrate a QC's elevation to the Bench.

Producer Chris Kelly says: 'A successful set of chambers may have 30 or 40 members, perhaps eight of whom will be "silks". Of those, a small minority may be women. A senior clerk told me that, 40 years ago, there wasn't one woman in any capacity in chambers. The number is growing, and now some solicitors positively discriminate in favour of women. However, in this male-dominated environment, female barristers often complain of sexism – particularly from senior clerks, some of whom make it plain that they'd rather deal with men – and also from arrogant ex-public school barristers. I read a survey recently which said that 45 per cent of women barristers complained of sexual harassment. These are supposed to be educated people in chambers, so I found that a bit dismaying. There's no doubt about it – even today, women have a tough time in chambers. And at first they get all the dogsbody work. Racism and class prejudice are also alive and well in chambers.

“I read a survey recently which said that 45 per cent of women barristers complained of sexual harassment”

BARRISTERS ADHERE TO AN ELABORATE CODE OF CONVENTIONS.

'It's not at all uncommon for a married male member of chambers to be having an affair with an unmarried female barrister in the same set, even if she's a pupil. In such cases, there are considerable complications, particularly for the pupil, whose chances of a tenancy may be sacrificed in order to preserve the "good name" of chambers. When I was conducting my research, I heard about a young female barrister having an affair with a married male barrister and interestingly they found themselves representing opposite sides in a divorce case!

'Marriage itself is a frequent casualty in chambers, where ever-greater pressures to succeed mean long working hours and weeks. I've heard of senior barristers who regularly ring home at 8pm – bath-time – to say goodnight to their children. That's a bit sad. Not surprisingly, enthusiastic drinking after work is a popular means of unwinding.

'The world of a London-based advocate is surprisingly small. People are thrown together – sometimes literally. Another story I was told concerned a married pupil who had a tryst in a broom cupboard with a married barrister...until they were discovered by the senior clerk.

'Some barristers turn to Law comparatively late in life. I came across one who had been a headmaster and another who had been British Airways' first female pilot.'

Barristers conform to an elaborate code of conventions – some useful, others merely traditional. For example, barristers don't shake hands with one another. Their word, it is fondly alleged, is their bond. In court, they wear what is, in effect, a uniform of wig, gown and white bands at the neck. In chambers, they also dress uniformly. Women invariably wear black, while the men wear dark suits. QCs wear elegant black silk suits, which is the reason they're known as 'silks'.

“Advocates often defend clients whom they strongly suspect are guilty”

Chris Kelly continues: 'While the job of the barrister is a thicket of ethics (the rules of evidence, for instance, occupy a volume as fat as the London Telephone Directory), it hasn't got much to do with conventional morality. Advocates often defend clients whom they strongly suspect are guilty. If they didn't, the adversarial system obviously couldn't work. But if a client were actually to tell his or her defence counsel that he or she was guilty, the barrister would be obliged to withdraw from the case.

'Some people like to compare advocates to medieval champions, bound loyally to defend or prosecute without undue regard for the rights or wrongs of the matter. Their primary aim is not even to elicit the truth of a case – it is to do their best for their client, whether it be an individual, an organisation or the Crown. It is then down to the twelve members of the jury, advised by the judge, to decide precisely where the truth lies.'

But the real power in chambers lies neither with the Head of Chambers nor the assembled barristers. It lies with the senior clerk. Chris Kelly says: 'The senior clerk's position is similar to that of a sergeant major – relatively modest in rank but high in influence. In the chambers, which we researched, the senior clerk tends to be a male Londoner, who didn't go on to higher education and whose family had links with chambers. He acts as the barristers' agent, attracting work from perhaps hundreds of solicitors and allocating it to members of chambers. He is later responsible for pursuing the solicitors to pay the barristers' fees. He will nurture the careers of those barristers he favours, but woe betide anyone foolish enough to cross him. Aldermarten once described Tom Buckley, our senior clerk, as the sort of person to be found at the other end of a pitbull terrier. Buckley is fairly typical of the breed. In extreme cases of dislike, it has been known for a senior clerk to starve a barrister of briefs and effectively force him out of chambers.

JOHN THAW DISCUSSES THE SCRIPT WITH PRODUCER CHRIS KELLY.

'The senior clerk also fixes the fees. Until fairly recently, his reward was up to 10 per cent of the income of chambers, and the income of an averagely successful, non-commercial set might be £5 million. Most chambers now pay a salary plus a smaller percentage, but plenty of senior clerks will still be earning around £200,000. Some sets are replacing their senior clerks with practice managers, who are often better educated (though not necessarily better at the job) and certainly much cheaper.

'Senior clerks make big money and, in many ways, rule the roost but, this being England, they are allowed no illusions about equality. While the barristers call them by their christian names, they in turn address members of chambers by their surnames. And, although they might all mix in the pub after work, senior clerks are not allowed to sit with barristers at formal occasions. Some senior clerks quietly resent this, but the majority couldn't care less. In the meantime, they have their own association whose meetings are legendarily riotous.'

SENIOR CLERKS SUCH AS TOM BUCKLEY CAN RULE THE ROOST IN CHAMBERS.

Matthew Hall, who has written two episodes for the second series of *Kavanagh Q.C.*, is ideally qualified to comment on life in chambers and in the courtroom. After studying Law at Oxford, he was a barrister for five years before turning to writing. What's more, his father-in-law is a Court of Appeal judge in Belfast, and his stepfather is TV dramatist GF Newman, responsible for such controversial programmes as the 1978 legal series *Law and Order*, whose provocative depiction of police corruption resulted in the Prison Officers' Association banning the BBC from filming inside jails for a year.

'I have been interested in creative writing for some time,' says 28-year-old Matthew, 'and, from my stepfather, I knew about the mechanics. I found the Law rather stifling – you have to think in a rigid way. Anyway, I had an idea for a story about a young barrister whose client dies in his cell in magistrates' court. It was based on the experience of someone I knew. It was called 'The Game' and it was the first thing I'd written for television. It ended up at Central and, on the strength of it, Chris Kelly commissioned me to do two episodes for *Kavanagh Q.C.*

KAVANAGH IS SEEN AS A GOOD ADVERT FOR THE LEGAL PROFESSION.

'One of the things I had to do was tone things down a bit for Kavanagh. In reality, criminal barristers are very flippant – it acts as a defence mechanism to prevent them from getting too involved emotionally in cases. While they appear terribly pompous in public, they swear like troopers in private.

'Barristers are often very brisk with clients and a lot have a rather uncaring attitude, again partly because they can't become too involved. As for juniors, they concentrate on staying awake through cases! They sometimes only get the papers the night before, and usually find themselves handling a number of cases at any one time. I did something like 50 to 60 per cent criminal work, the rest civil. Some barristers I knew hardly went to court at all and I must confess I didn't really like court.

'Barristers approve of Kavanagh – they say it is very close to reality. And he himself is pretty straight, a good advert for the profession. Obviously having been on both sides of the fence, I can see the odd discrepancy but, for my part, I've tried to be true to life. It's fair to say that the series sticks to rigid courtroom etiquette more than exists in reality – there are fewer outbursts than really happen. And the judges are slightly different too. In reality, judges are always butting in and barristers are very much aware of the judge's personality. If they get too passionate in their defence speeches, they are liable to be pulled up by the judge.

“In reality, criminal barristers are very flippant...”

'And I have to say that judges are far more pompous and absurd than would look realistic on television. Nobody would believe some of the things they say. I remember in a case of mine the judge suddenly demanded: “What is a kebab?” Some of them are frighteningly out-of-touch.

'Television also has to speed up courtroom proceedings considerably because most days in court are like watching paint dry. Court can be very boring with hours on end being spent arguing points of law. And at the end of the day, in my experience, juries are swayed more by emotion than by evidence.

'There is a lot of backroom bargaining between lawyers and in truth lawyers are very friendly with each other, a fact which, although it can annoy clients, actually operates to defendants' advantage. A lot of clients don't trust their barrister and perceive him or her as being no different from the police. Young clients, in particular, won't always co-operate. That mistrust, coupled with a police murder and a false confession, formed the basis for one of my Kavanagh episodes. The other one, 'Men of Substance', was an amalgam of various drugs trials I've been involved with. So I was able to base it on fact – the way drugs are concealed in secret compartments, how the operations are invariably fronted by apparently legitimate businesses, even the bent customs officer. They certainly exist.

'Although I've been a barrister, I want to take a certain amount of dramatic licence and this sometimes leads to a good-natured difference of opinion with the show's legal adviser, David Bradly. We argue about things such as the way Kavanagh examines his own witnesses. You can be as vicious as you like in cross-examination, but you can only prompt your own witnesses. You're not allowed to put words into their mouths – you can't ask questions where the answer can be a simple "yes" or "no". It all makes for a very difficult writing exercise, trying to prevent the speeches from sounding too banal, while endeavouring to retain that essential authenticity. It's a case of attempting to be accurate but dramatic.'

“ Barristers approve of Kavanagh – they say it is very close to reality ”

Amidst all the plaudits which have come Kavanagh's way regarding authenticity, one error slipped through the net and was gleefully seized upon by a member of the legal profession in a letter to the Times. The correspondent pointed out that a judge had been seen entering a crown court improperly dressed, minus the red sash worn de rigueur in criminal cases.

Chris Kelly admits: 'It was one of those things. We had judges writing to the *Times*, saying: "We thoroughly enjoy the series, but..." '

ALDERMARTEN LIVES TO REGRET HIS DECISION TO DEFEND CON-WOMAN LUCY CARTWRIGHT.

Chapter Four

James Joseph Kavanagh Q.C.

James Kavanagh was born and raised in a small terraced house in the old Lancashire mill town of Bolton. On a clear day – and there weren't many of those – you could see Manchester. London might as well have been on another planet.

Right: Kavanagh's love of the law began when he visited Crown Court aged 16.

His father, Alf, was a minor trade union official, not because he enjoyed the work but because he considered it an obligation. Alf and his wife, Marjorie, are homely folk and, even now in their late seventies, still live in that same terraced house.

One of three children, young James had always appeared the most likely to succeed. He was a bright lad, which was a mystery to his parents who had instilled in him good manners but left the rest of his development to chance. James was educated at the local grammar school and Nottingham University, where he read Law, played football, climbed in the Peak District and, at the home of a rich friend, learned to sail. While at university, he took a part-time job in a bowling alley to subsidise his meagre spending money.

Above: Julia hangs on Kavanagh's every word.

His love of all things legal dates back to his 16th birthday when, on impulse, his father took him to Manchester Crown Court. The subdued sense of drama, the impression that great issues were being decided and the clarity of the arguments were a revelation to him. From that moment on, there was never any doubt in his mind about where his future lay.

Kavanagh was called to the Bar at the age of 25, beginning his legal career as a pupil at 5 River Court, Middle Temple, where he is now a leading luminary. The initial period of financial hardship proved a strain and, contrary to the strict rules, he resorted to moon-

lighting at nights as a minicab driver, all the while terrified that he might be spotted by a member of chambers. This would have provided some people with just the ammunition they needed to show him the door. For, still largely the domain of the upper middle classes, the Inns of Court regarded most newcomers from Kavanagh's background as mere upstarts – at least until they had proved themselves. This the determined Kavanagh soon did. Once successful, he never forgot the condescension of the worst of the old guard. Whilst he harbours no bitterness towards them, he is not easily disposed to forgive and forget.

“...financial hardship proved a strain...he resorted to moonlighting at nights as a minicab driver”

Kavanagh met his wife, Lizzie Probyn, in the Sixties, when she was a member of the pro-abortion lobby and he was a hungry junior with a reputation as a radical. His successful, at times impassioned, defence of her cause won the day and, suitably impressed, Lizzie asked him to join her for a drink in the pub. It wasn't until shortly before the wedding, two months later, that he learned she was the daughter of a life peer, Lord Probyn.

With his staunch left-wing views, Alf Kavanagh took a while to come to terms with the fact that a son of his was marrying into the aristocracy. This was one union Alf did not wholly approve of and, for a while, he and Marjorie referred to it, somewhat disparagingly, as 'that marriage'. But when they realised that neither Lizzie nor London had robbed James of his northern warmth and down-to-earth approach, they were happy to welcome Lizzie into the fold.

THE KAVANAGHS' BUSY SCHEDULES ALLOW THEM VERY LITTLE TIME TOGETHER AS A FAMILY.

They're very proud of Kavanagh, although they only express it in an oblique way. He doesn't see them very often these days, but his parents are immensely important to him. Fundamentally, their values remain his.

Kavanagh and Lizzie have two children, Kate (18) and Matt (16). They live in a handsome period detached house in Barnes, with a large garden and views over green spaces. This material achievement is a source of pride to Kavanagh. Unlike some barristers, he has friends outside chambers – people with wide interests and a lively sense of the ridiculous. When time permits, he sails a beautifully-restored elderly Nicholson sloop, moored at Pin Mill, near Ipswich.

Kavanagh 'took silk' nine years ago and he has since established himself as one of the most respected criminal advocates in London. His rapier-like cross-examination, patient and relentless, is admired by colleagues and opponents alike, as is his liberal commitment to clients and causes which are far from universally popular. Sympathetic to the aspirations of minorities, he has been known to take on cases for minimal reward. This doesn't go down well with his senior clerk, but Kavanagh insists it's the occasional price barristers should pay for their privileges.

Kavanagh undoubtedly has the ability to be on the Bench but this would remove him from where he feels he really belongs – in combat on the floor of the courtroom.

KATE AND MATT, THE KAVANAGHS' TEENAGE CHILDREN.

JOHN THAW

as James Kavanagh Q.C.

Just as James Kavanagh has conquered the British legal system from unlikely beginnings in a terraced house in Bolton, so John Thaw has risen to become one of our most acclaimed actors from a similarly humble background.

JOHN THAW AS KAVANAGH WITH TOM BRODIE AS SON MATT.

John dislikes comparisons between himself and the characters he plays, but concedes that Kavanagh's upbringing was one of the attractions of the part. 'Ted Childs, Chris Kelly and I had a meeting about what sort of character he was and where he had come from. Ted and Chris suggested that he was from northern, working-class origins and that appealed to me, particularly as I come from the same background.'

John Thaw was born in Manchester on January 3, 1942, the son of a lorry driver. The family lived in a small council flat in the suburb of Longsight but, when John was six, his mother left home, and, with his father often working unsociable hours, John was left to look after younger brother Raymond. 'I had to get back and cook the meal after school, when my dad was away, and make sure Raymond didn't come home to an empty house. It gave me a sense of responsibility from early on.'

By the age of 12, John was amusing friends with Max Miller impersonations. 'Then I got the role of Mistress Quickly in *Henry IV Part One* at school. I seemed to have a talent for acting and I liked it. The headmaster encouraged me to pursue it, but someone from my background had no idea how to become an actor.'

In the meantime, John left school at 16 with one 'O' Level and went to work in Manchester fruit market, weighing apples and pears. 'The early starts were a killer and, to make matters worse, I worked for a guy who wanted to be the last stall to close. So it made for a really long day.'

John's sights were still fixed firmly on acting, however. 'Eventually, I met some people at a youth club, who knew the ropes, and I decided I had to get an audition at RADA. My dad was marvellous about it. He said it was worth having a go and, if I failed, I could come home and he and Ray would be there. So, I knew I had that sort of security behind me.'

By the time the audition came around, John was working as a baker's apprentice. He took the day off work and drove to London with his dad, arriving at RADA looking, he thought, like the bees knees. 'I was wearing tight trousers and a Teddy Boy haircut and thought I looked pretty good. It was the height of fashion for Manchester but, of course, all the RADA students were very laid back. I was really out of place.'

Fortunately, RADA accepted Teddy Boys too and John soon found himself in a class with, among others, Tom Courtenay and Sarah Miles. 'It was a different world,' he reflects, 'scary, not quite what I'd imagined. There was more to it than getting up and showing off, learning the technique and things like that. In the first term, I was all at sea – not very good. I think it was touch and go whether they kept me on, but I was determined to work harder and get better in the second term.'

"John left school at 16 with one "O" Level and went to work in Manchester fruit market"

He succeeded to the extent that, on leaving RADA with an award, he went straight into repertory at Liverpool. His stage debut, somewhat prophetically as it turned out, was as a uniformed police officer. John then moved down to London and shared a flat with Tom Courtenay, while carving out a career for himself. As with all young actors, he had his share of disappointments, notably missing out on the opportunity to succeed Ron Moody as Fagin in *Oliver!* But television producers had started to notice his extraordinary

KAVANAGH AND LIZZIE CHEER ON MATT AT A SCHOOL SWIMMING GALA.

talent and he made his television debut in a play entitled *Flow Gently Sweet Afton*. 'It sounds terribly arty, doesn't it? It was all set in Southend!'

At 21, he understudied Laurence Olivier in a West End production of *Semi-Detached*. When Olivier decided to take a week off, John stepped into the role of playing a 60-year-old, carrying it off with remarkable aplomb. During the run, he met Sally Alexander, then an assistant stage manager, and soon they were married with a daughter, Abigail.

“I was once told I wouldn't come into my own until I was in my forties – and it's been quite true”

John's big break came in 1964, when he was cast as no-nonsense military police sergeant John Mann in 26 episodes of the ABC series *Redcap*. The story editor on *Redcap* was Ian Kennedy Martin, who would later create the television series which first made John Thaw a household name, *The Sweeney*.

'I was once told I wouldn't come into my own until I was in my forties – and it's been quite true. But it was a bit daunting at the time. I was about 17 or 18 and I thought I'd have to survive for 20 years before I started making a living. Then at 22, along came *Redcap*. My name was above the title and I thought that, whoever had said that about me waiting till I was 40, was wrong. Then at 26, I was out of work for nine months, and it all came back.'

By 1968, John's marriage to Sally had broken up and he was sharing a London flat with actor Nicol Williamson. While out of work, he took to strolling in Kensington Gardens. Nine months later, he landed a part in *The Borderers* as a hard-drinking, lawless Scottish aristocrat, who wore a lot of hair lacquer and lunged at wenches. John Thaw has never looked back since.

One role was in the stage play *So What About Love?*, which co-starred Sheila Hancock. They married on Christmas Eve 1973. But it was television that was to prove John's forte with productions such as the Dick Clement and Ian La Frenais sitcom *Thick*

BOTH KAVANAGH AND LIZZIE SEEM PREOCCUPIED WITH THEIR OWN TRAINS OF THOUGHT.

as Thieves (with Bob Hoskins), *The Sweeney*, Sir Francis Drake in *Drake's Venture*, the newspaper drama *Mitch* and another turn at comedy as harassed parent Henry Willows in *Home to Roost*.

Unlike many actors who yearn to return to the stage, John enjoys television as a medium. 'I've played many of the classics on stage with the Royal Shakespeare Company and the National Theatre – things like Tom Stoppard's *Night and Day* with Diana Rigg, Sergeant Musgrave in *Sergeant Musgrave's Dance* and Sir Toby Belch in *Twelfth Night* – but the thing I like about television is the risk element of never having said those lines before, never having opened that door before or sat in that chair before. Can I make somebody sitting at home believe that I am this character, saying these lines as if I've just thought of them? For me, that's more difficult than going on stage every night.'

John has fond memories of Jack Regan in *The Sweeney* and jokes that, if ITV had their way, he and co-star Dennis Waterman would still be doing it now! 'But after four years, Dennis and I both decided enough was enough.'

The Sweeney came under fire from certain quarters for being too violent. John defends it to the hilt. 'We didn't have nudity but we did have swearing and violence. It wasn't gratuitous because it was about the Flying Squad and that, sadly, was par for the course. If I believed that my roughing someone up in *The Sweeney* made a viewer go out and copy what they'd seen me do, I'd never have made the programme in the first place. We showed violent scenes because that's the sort of thing the Flying Squad encounter every day of their working lives. If they go out to arrest a villain, they don't say to him: "Would you mind accompanying me to the station?" '

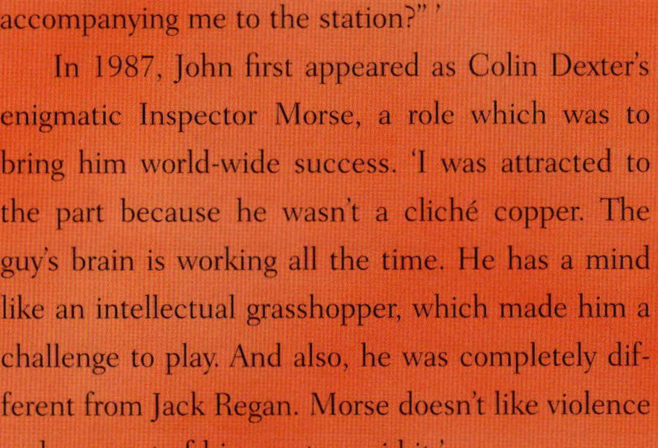

THE KAVANAGHS' MARRIAGE ISN'T ALWAYS PLAIN SAILING DUE TO THEIR CLASHING CAREER COMMITMENTS.

In 1987, John first appeared as Colin Dexter's enigmatic Inspector Morse, a role which was to bring him world-wide success. 'I was attracted to the part because he wasn't a cliché copper. The guy's brain is working all the time. He has a mind like an intellectual grasshopper, which made him a challenge to play. And also, he was completely different from Jack Regan. Morse doesn't like violence and goes out of his way to avoid it.'

"If I believed that my roughing someone up in *The Sweeney* made a viewer go out and copy what they'd seen me do, I'd never have made the programme in the first place"

Sold to over fifty countries and with a British audience of around 18 million, *Inspector Morse* was the most popular drama series of its day. John's only reservation was that he hated the real ale which was Morse's favourite tipple. 'Every time we had to shoot a scene in a pub where I was supposed to be drinking, I tried to make sure I was seen just downing the last few drops of a pint.'

He was also, he says, acutely embarrassed to read articles dubbing him a sex symbol. 'There was something in the press at the time saying I was one of the sexiest men on television – or some such rubbish – and Sheila and the girls all laughed and took the mickey, quite rightly. What they mean is that Morse is sexy, not me. I used to get lots of letters from women on *The Sweeney*, as I did on Morse, and, although they all started "Dear John", those women were really writing to Regan or Morse.'

“There was something in the press saying I was one of the sexiest men on television”

However he can appreciate why women have found Morse so attractive. 'It's nothing to do with the way he looks – just the way he is. He likes women, he's sensitive and romantic, and he doesn't hide it if he's attracted to someone, but he's also a challenge. Women see him as the eternal bachelor: they think they can change him, but he's so set in his ways it's impossible.'

Between series of Morse, John busied himself with other projects, including the role of Bomber Harris in the BBC drama about the leader of Bomber Command. His portrayal brought praise from Harris' family and the Bomber Command Association.

All good things come to an end and, after five years, Morse reached the limit of its

LIZZIE AND KAVANAGH ENJOY A QUIET MOMENT TOGETHER AT HOME.

natural lifespan as a series, although John did agree to star in a one-off special. Ted Childs, his producer on *The Sweeney* and executive producer on *Inspector Morse*, was understandably keen to sign John up for a new project. Ted's idea was for a liberal barrister and he steadily set about overcoming John's initial misgivings about wearing a wig. John finally agreed while he was at the National Theatre playing Labour Party leader, the Right Honourable George Jones, in David Hare's play *The Absence of War*.

THE KAVANAGHS MAKE THE MOST OF AN OPPORTUNITY TO HAVE A MEAL TOGETHER.

'I was committed to the series before I saw a script,' says John, 'that being Ted's way, but I trusted Ted implicitly regarding the quality. So when Russell Lewis' script arrived, I was well pleased. Kavanagh is a totally different person from Morse. If he hadn't been, I wouldn't have taken him on. For one thing, although he is obviously part of the Law, he has little or no direct contact with the police. Also, he's a family man and he's from the north, so I've given him a Manchester accent. I couldn't just bring back my old accent – it would be too unbelievable. It was so thick. Kavanagh has lived in the south for 25 to 30 years, so I decided just to flatten out the vowels because, unlike an actor, the guy doesn't have to lose his accent.

'Kavanagh is one thing professionally, but something different altogether in his private life. In that respect, he's like everyone else who has any sort of job. The idea of having two career people – Kavanagh and Lizzie – is very relevant to marriage today. His life is the Law, to the extent that his wife was having an affair with another barrister because Kavanagh had been neglecting his duties at home. Similarly, the problems the Kavanaghs face with teenage kids are typical of many people. It's very worrying these days for parents.

“Kavanagh is one thing professionally, but something different altogether in his private life”

'The Kavanaghs are now trying to rebuild the marriage, which was why he passed up the chance to become Head of Chambers. I'd hire him. He's not over the top like Rumpole and, we hope, he isn't exactly like every barrister hero there's ever been. He's a liberal man, who believes in fairness. And he's climbed to the top of an elite profession, to become one of the country's leading advocates, through sheer hard work and a love of the Law.'

To research the role, John visited the Inns of Court and attended a murder trial at the Old Bailey. 'Although the script is all there for you, I like to observe human behaviour and to ask a lot of questions.

'Strangely enough, I've never played a barrister before. Indeed, I'd only ever been to court once in my life before and that was as a witness at magistrates' court in the case of a man who left the scene of an accident. I remember, when I was giving evidence, I was made to feel like I was the one on trial, that I was being prosecuted – because he had this sharp barrister. So I understand why people get terribly wary and nervous about being witnesses. Barristers can be frightening. All in all, it was not a happy experience – particularly since the bloke got off.

'So meeting barristers was a new experience for me. I found them very interesting guys, very bright, very amusing and very quick. And that's what Kavanagh is in terms of his work – he has a clear, logical mind. But, unlike some, Kavanagh can put it over to the jury. His speeches really play to the jury. They're hard work because you're speaking in a jargon and people don't usually speak like that. So the actual learning process is twice as hard as doing something like Morse. That I find a bit of a burden.

AMONG THE IMPRESSIVE ARRAY OF GUEST STARS IN SERIES TWO IS MICHAEL WILLIAMS.

'I said to Chris Kelly over lunch just before we started filming the second series that the court stuff is not my favourite thing, to say the least. But that is what the series is about and my job – because I think of acting as a job – is to entertain. And, if people are entertained by the courtroom scenes, then it doesn't matter what I go through, as long as the end product is successful.

'It's no secret that I don't like the wigs and gowns. Courtrooms as a whole are dreadful – I can see why judges get so ratty. In hot weather, they are airless places and, of course, you are stuck in one place and pretty well the same position. I now understand why they adjourn at 3.30pm. It's all they can take! Unfortunately, we couldn't adjourn until seven or eight at night.'

Does John see any similarities between being a barrister and an actor? 'I've heard of barristers who admit to feeling different when they put on what I call the uniform of the wig and gown. They say they feel different, and that suggests to me that they're playing a role. I think that's why the majority voted to keep the wigs and so on, because they actually get a buzz out of the preparation, putting on the wing collar, the tabs, the gown and the wig. It's a sort of ritual. The jury are their audience. Barristers are out to impress the jury and, to a lesser extent, the judge with their skills. So, to that extent, there is a link between acting and being a barrister.'

John was delighted that Mike Mansfield QC unwittingly vindicated his decision to give Kavanagh long hair. 'When I saw Mike Mansfield – I didn't get a chance to speak to him – he had longer hair than any barrister I'd seen. I wanted long hair anyway and used Mansfield as an excuse. If people had said to me, barristers don't have long hair, I'd have probably backed down but, having seen Mansfield, I thought, well, he's got long hair down to his collar, so we can do that.

'We've been very fortunate in having a real barrister, David Bradly, as our legal adviser. When David's around, I can ask him about various points. He's very helpful and also understands the fact that, although we try to be as realistic as we can, there are times when we have to cut corners to make it entertaining. It has to be a compromise, although I must say Kavanagh has been less of a compromise than some police shows.

'The legal stuff has been adhered to closely. Recently, we had a retired judge on the set to have a look round just because he liked the series. He said it was the most realistic legal series he'd seen. And in fact the response from the public to Kavanagh was actually better than when we first did Morse.'

JOHN THAW TREADS THE BOARDS ON HMS VICTORY.

John Thaw has every reason to be happy with life. Two years ago, he and his wife Sheila moved out of London to an 18th century Wiltshire manor house, where he is able to indulge his passion for growing roses. Daughters Abigail and Melanie are both established actresses, while the youngest, Joanna, has been studying at Cambridge. 'She has no plans to become an actress. I think she's going to do a proper job,' laughs John. 'I never encouraged the other two. Acting is the dodgiest profession on the face of the earth.

'For my part, I couldn't have been anything other than an actor. I'm a very shy person and perhaps acting was my way of coping with life. It's worked. I'm much better now, although I think most shy people get less shy as they get older. I'm very comfortable with my life now. I'm a very lucky man.'

> **“the response from the public to Kavanagh was actually better than when we first did Morse”**

He remains the most unassuming of actors, as baffled by the deluge of praise that has been heaped on him over the years as he was by the absurd over-reaction to the disappointing ratings for the TV adaptation of Peter Mayle's *A Year in Provence*. 'I never get big-headed about acting,' he says. 'It's just a job. I've been in this game for over 30 years and, if I can't tell the difference now between what is my job and what is my real life, I never will. I've had praise and prizes, and there's no way I believe all the hype.'

In 1991, the British Film Institute ran a retrospective of his work. When his agent rang to tell him about the accolade, John Thaw was typically stunned with disbelief. 'I thought I must have died and nobody had bothered to tell me! I thought the whole thing was a wind-up...'

Chapter Five

Family and colleagues

Since most of the characters in Kavanagh Q.C. reappear each week, the series does contain serial elements – such as Kate Kavanagh's ongoing relationship with boyfriend Luke in the first run.

'But,' says producer Chris Kelly, 'the aim is to keep these to a minimum so that each episode is capable of standing alone. Underlying the main action in each episode, which is obviously the court case, is a strong sense of life and internal politics in chambers. And we also keep Kavanagh's family, particularly his wife Lizzie, very much in the frame. Apart from any other consideration, they're virtually the only "civilians" with whom Kavanagh has a chance to discuss his doubts and preoccupations. We've developed his private life as a continuing sub-plot, especially where it relates to his work and vice-versa. His relationship with Lizzie, not entirely harmonious at the very start of the series, is as much a pointer to the man and his strengths and weaknesses as his work.

It's not easy to incorporate a domestic story which can be sympathetic to the main story without overbalancing it. We certainly don't want to get too soapy – that's not what people expect or want from *Kavanagh Q.C.*'

KAVANAGH WITH HIS FAMILY – THE DOMESTIC SIDE OF THE BUSY Q.C. IS ESSENTIAL TO THE SERIES.

LISA HARROW

as Lizzie Kavanagh

New Zealand-born actress Lisa Harrow can see certain similarities between her own marriage and that of Lizzie Kavanagh.

Four years ago, Lisa married American marine biologist Roger Payne, whose work takes him off around the world for months on end. And the Kavanaghs are constantly trying to juggle two careers. Lisa says: 'I live with exactly the same problem as Lizzie – two careers. Roger is in demand world-wide. If we wanted to, we could travel all year. But he doesn't want my career to suffer in any way.

'For example, just as Roger and I had fixed our wedding and honeymoon, I was offered a television series with filming beginning five days after we were due to get married. It seemed too good an opportunity to turn down. Roger generously said I should take it. So, after we got married in Vermont, I flew back to London to begin work while Roger flew to Alaska and had our honeymoon with my son Timmy.

“ In Kavanagh, two very high-powered people are trying to sustain a relationship ”

'They spent three weeks on a boat in the middle of nowhere filming humpback whales, and on land they went looking for bears together. Every evening, they curled up together and Roger read Timmy *Treasure Island*. Then they used to ring me on the radio telephone and tell me what a good time they were having and how they missed me.

'We were due to spend six months together at Roger's house in the States last year but then I was offered a part in the play *In Praise of Love*. I love theatre but felt we'd spent enough time doing what I wanted, so I was going to turn it down. Roger told me I'd be mad not to take it.

'Once when I was doing a play in Southampton, he drove me there every day and saw every performance. He would then spend the rest of the evening in a call box ringing round the world.

LISA HARROW IS LIZZIE KAVANAGH – A WOMAN JUGGLING A CAREER AND A FAMILY.

'It is hard when two people have jobs of equal importance and have to balance out a life together. In Kavanagh, two very high-powered people are trying to sustain a relationship. In the TV show, I'm keen to examine the stress that two successful, hardworking partners puts on a relationship. These days, more and more women are into careers rather than being the little woman at home. The question is: Whose job takes priority?'

Lizzie Kavanagh is a few years younger than her husband. She is an intelligent, positive and attractive woman, who doesn't suffer fools gladly. Educated at London University, where she read Modern Languages, she was politically active on the left in her twenties and remains a socialist, although she is beginning to wonder whether the Labour Party has completely abandoned the ideals which made her join it.

“When Lizzie first met Kavanagh, she found both his principles and his sense of humour powerfully attractive”

She comes from a wealthy background. Her father, Lord Probyn, was given a life peerage for services to engineering – he set up a successful construction company, Probyn Roadstone – and to the Conservative Party. Despite his devotion to Margaret Thatcher, Lizzie gets on well with her father. Her mother died five years ago.

When Lizzie first met Kavanagh, she found both his principles and his sense of humour powerfully attractive. She also loved the fact that he had none of the familiar middle-class woolly-mindedness about him. Kavanagh knew where he was going but, unlike most men she met, he wasn't going there just for the money or the kudos. He believed he could do something useful. Lizzie still loves those qualities – but there has been a price to pay.

Feeling that she was coming a poor second to Kavanagh's work, Lizzie embarked on a brief affair with his fellow barrister, Miles Petersham. At the time, Kavanagh was working six days a week. He became distracted, over-tired, inattentive and began taking Lizzie for granted, behaving more like a lodger than a lover. Sex was perfunctory, infrequent and, for Lizzie, unfulfilling. Miles, by contrast, was attentive, attractive, obviously physically excited by her, but at the same time not a long-term threat to her marriage. In a moment of weakness, she made love with him while Kavanagh was up north, and found the experience exhilarating. Miles made her feel like Kavanagh used to – desirable, needed, satisfied. Although the physical sensations had rejuvenated Lizzie, before long Miles' shallowness began to make his company pall.

Lizzie wasn't consumed by guilt, except in so far as Kavanagh was hurt and to some extent humiliated. Miles had been a friend of his and London law is a small community. The wound has now healed but Kavanagh and Lizzie know they must never drift apart again. However she won't make the process easy by being the submissive, remorseful wife. Kavanagh must meet her halfway.

She worked for a charity which administers the funds of a trust set up to help sick and needy children world-wide. An excellent fund-raiser who does not allow her emotions to cloud her judgement, she was offered a post in Strasbourg. Both she and her husband knew this would mean another lengthy separation but were determined to make the relationship work this time. Even so, it was with some relief that Kavanagh welcomed her back into the fold after the job proved something of a disappointment. Still, she didn't let the grass grow under her feet, however, and was soon appointed fund-raiser for a large hospital project.

'She's a very forceful, independent woman,' says Lisa, 'and, despite past hiccups, she and Kavanagh have a warm, loving relationship. She works hard but at the same time manages to hold the family together.'

In real life, Lisa's own marriage to Roger followed a whirlwind romance. They were brought together by their love of the environment.

'Greenpeace asked me to talk at a rally in Trafalgar Square about whales,' says Lisa. 'My speech included some of Roger's theories on whale communication, and afterwards he came and spoke to me. We carried on talking for several hours. I fell in love with him there and then. When we finally parted, I thought to myself: "I'm going to marry that man."'

DIRECTOR CHARLES BEESON (RIGHT) GOES THROUGH THE SCRIPT WITH NICHOLAS JONES, JOHN THAW AND LISA HARROW.

The day after their first meeting, Roger took Lisa and her eight-year-old son Timmy (from a previous relationship with Australian actor Sam Neill) to the zoo. Then he went to Iceland and wrote to Lisa from there. On another flying visit to London, he asked Timmy for Lisa's hand in marriage and within 10 weeks of their first meeting, Lisa and Roger were married.

JOHN THAW AND LISA HARROW OUTSIDE THE INNS OF COURT.

'We'd only spent a total of two weeks together at that point,' Lisa reflects, 'so getting married was an enormous act of faith.'

Despite their hectic schedules, Lisa and Roger have since managed to spend a fair amount of time together. Roger, who gave the world the first recording of the songs of humpback whales, has a research station in Patagonia where white whales are observed.

'It's an amazing place,' says Lisa. 'You get a feeling of being totally at one with the elements. There's no telephone, no music, simply the earth and its inhabitants. So you sit for hours watching an eagle in a nest or listening to the noises of the whales, and it's only afterwards that you realise what a beautiful, calming way it is to spend time and to understand something new about life.

'If you're married, you should spend time together but with Timmy at school in this country, it's been difficult. I'm certainly interested in spending more time on the work that Roger's doing and in working alongside him. My skills as a communicator could be invaluable. We're thinking about how we can use his skills with mine to illuminate environmental issues but, at the same time, be entertaining as well. We want to talk to hearts and minds without being too didactic. The whole of the globe needs to be spoken for.

'Seeing whales changes you because you realise that out there are things which are so huge, so majestic, and they live a life which doesn't touch ours. When they fling themselves out of the water, it takes your breath away.'

Has Lisa ever considered a job exchange with her husband? 'I couldn't,' she smiles, 'because he knows so much. But he wants me to go with him. He's not at all exclusive about what he does.'

Lisa Harrow was born 51 years ago in Auckland. 'My first acting role was a performance of *Alice in Wonderland* in our garage. I was about six and my brother played the White Rabbit. I did quite a few plays at school and we had a teacher who used to write little musical pieces for us.'

She later joined a children's theatre group and, convinced that acting was her vocation, came to Britain in 1966 to try her luck. At the time, the New Zealand government was giving budding artists bursaries to study abroad.

'It's the same type of bursary that Kiri Te Kanawa came over on and we were both very lucky to get them because the government are now using the money to try and set up theatre companies in New Zealand instead.

'At the age of 10, I had dreamed of acting Shakespeare at Stratford but I thought it was impossible. So when I went straight to the Royal Shakespeare Company from drama school, it was a dream come true.'

Lisa spent four years with the RSC and has since appeared in countless television, film and stage productions, including *Nancy Astor, A Sense of Guilt*, Ruth Rendell's The *Strawberry Tree, Act of Betrayal* and *The Last Days of Chez Nous*, for which she won the Australian Best Actress Award.

“My first acting role was a performance of Alice in Wonderland in our garage”

'Lizzie Kavanagh is probably one of the most glamorous parts I've played. It's also just about the first time I've not played the central role in a series. It's rather nice not to have that responsibility because it gives me time to live my life which means I can devote more energy to my son and husband. It's good to do a job that's high-profile, well respected and with good production values but at the same time knowing that John Thaw's doing all the work. I just come in from time to time, look gorgeous and walk away again!

'John and I have worked together before on an episode of *Inspector Morse*. I was the wife of a murder victim. John and I had a big scene together by a swimming pool – I did a lot of swimming in that story.

'I'm full of admiration for the way John learns his speeches in Kavanagh because it's frightfully dry, factual stuff and quite technical. I speak from experience because, although I've never been near a court in my life (I've been a good girl), I did do an episode of Crown Court when I was pregnant. I was a defence counsel, but I was waiting for the results of tests telling me whether or not my child would live and frankly, at the time, my mind was preoccupied with that. I thought I could get away with not learning my lines because I reckoned that, when you did a court scene, you could have all the words written down in front of you. But I was wrong. And in the end I had to learn them. So what I thought would be a doddle turned out to be considerably harder work. Needless to say, it's not something I've tried since.'

ANNA CHANCELLOR

as Julia Piper

Anna Chancellor has a confession to make. On screen as ambitious junior barrister Julia Piper, she may look cool and sophisticated but the truth is that, during last summer's heat wave, she got so hot that she was forced to play most of her scenes barefoot and without any tights!

'It was so hot, especially under the wigs and the layers of black, that I used to take my tights and shoes off. The top half of me looked posh and the lower half looked a mess. But it was no problem because they usually only film me from the waist up – they rarely show my feet. I did think about standing in a bowl of cold water but thought that might be going a bit too far...

'I found wearing the wig and gown in the courtroom scenes very uncomfortable because I'm naturally a scruffy person. I had the same problem when I played Miss Caroline Bingley in *Pride and Prejudice* because I had to sit around for ages in a corset. Once you were in it, you were in it all day. Some people are just naturally neat and immaculate and can sit for hours and not get a hair out of place. Not me!'

“I found wearing the wig and gown in the courtroom scenes very uncomfortable because I'm naturally a scruffy person”

At 29, Anna is one of the country's rising stars, her fame sealed by her role as Henrietta (Duck Face), the hapless fiancee who floored Hugh Grant after he had jilted her at the altar in *Four Weddings And A Funeral*. But Anna's rise has been far from conventional. On the way, she has had to cope with a young pregnancy, abject poverty and a 'neurotic nun'.

Anna was brought up in Somerset by her mother and stepfather. The youngest of three sisters, she insists that she has always wanted to be an actress – despite her childhood experiences at a convent at Shaftesbury, Dorset.

JULIA PIPER – HOLDS HER OWN IN A LEGAL WORLD DOMINATED BY MEN.

'At the age of 10, I was sent to the Institute of the Blessed Virgin Mary where I wasn't that good at studies but I loved being in the plays. I used to direct some of them too. But when it came to doing Shakespeare, one of the nuns, Sister Ursula, took charge. For some reason, she always hated me – except when it came to casting the school play. But she used to get into such a state directing these plays that I'm surprised it didn't kill her. Fortunately, there was another woman, our elocution teacher, who was a lot calmer. I think she saved our sanity.'

Anna's first role at convent was that of Elvira in *Blithe Spirit*, hotly pursued by Rosalind in *As You Like It*. 'I knew the whole play off by heart,' she recalls, 'including everyone else's part. I was that keen.

'I decided that I wanted to go to drama school but, of course, everybody thinks you're never going to make it. However, my mum was pleased that I had found something which would occupy me. Even I had my doubts and, when I did get to drama school, I thought I'd never have a job. I hated drama school. It was so bad that I nearly gave up acting there and then. It was a very tough regime. The idea is that they strip you down to build you up again but sometimes they forget to build you up again. They were very critical of me – they criticised the way I walked, the way I talked. I think they thought I was very privileged, that life had come too easily for me.'

"The key moment in her career was the hugely successful *Four Weddings And A Funeral*"

Anna's anguish was cut short when she met a poet called Jock Scott and became pregnant. In 1987, at the age of 21, she quit drama school to give birth to daughter Poppy.

'I never doubted that I wanted to have the baby – it must have been the force of motherhood or something – but it looked like everything had gone off the rails. I didn't know what would happen. I couldn't go out and work with a newborn baby. We didn't have any money and I remember feeling everyone had gone on ahead and that terrible feeling, which mothers get anyway, of feeling left out, trapped. It's a terrible thing to feel and I'd feel guilty if I ever thought that now.

'The baby was a fundamental turning point for me. She gave me something to focus on, something I had to do. I had to think of some way of earning a living, not just for myself but for my daughter too. And acting was the only thing I could do.

'I used to be so unsuccessful it was almost a joke. My posh pals used to laugh at me because I was broke. It was awful. One friend, a real Hooray Henry, told everyone my flat was disgusting. He said there were piles of nappies and duck mess everywhere. That was because we had a pet duck at the time.'

Meanwhile Anna's career was progressing slowly. She worked in repertory at Pitlochry in the Scottish Highlands for eight months, doing half a dozen plays. 'They were only small parts but at least they enabled me to get my Equity card. After that, the parts began to trickle in ... I was a hysterical wife in an episode of *Casualty*, I was an ecstasy dealer at an acid house rave in *Inspector Morse* (I didn't even get to meet John Thaw) and I was in an episode of *Poirot*. It was a flashback and I played Virginie, the only woman the great detective had ever loved. Luckily, I didn't have to kiss that moustache...'

Financially Anna's salvation came through a couple of commercials and one, for Boddington's beer, had even more far-reaching effects. For Anna fell in love with the cameraman, Nigel Willoughby, and they got married last year.

However, the key moment in her career was the hugely successful *Four Weddings And A Funeral*. 'I earned £12,000 for three weeks' work and have been working ever since. We had no idea when we were making it that it would be as big as it was. There was my name next to Kristen Scott Thomas, Simon Callow and Rowan Atkinson. I thought that if I could hold my head up with them and not stick out like a sore thumb, then that would be an achievement in itself. The only problem was that for months afterwards, people called me Duck Face. I used to want to scream!'

Anna says that the second series of Kavanagh will be her last. 'I've enjoyed myself enormously but I want to spread my wings. For girls in acting, the employment span is maybe not as long as it is with men. There aren't too many parts for older girls.'

When she looks back on *Kavanagh Q.C.* in years to come, Anna will always remember her performance in the annual chambers cricket match.

'I didn't know how to play cricket and, since Julia was supposed to be a demon bowler, they sent me off on a little bowling course at Wandsworth. The biggest problem was keeping my arm straight. I tended to throw which was a legacy from when I used to play netball.

'Funnily enough, when we came to do the first "take", they asked: "Are you ready to go?" I said: "OK, I'll have a go." I ran in, bowled, didn't even look where the ball had gone but celebrated as if I'd got the batsman out, which was what was supposed to happen in the story. Then I turned round and everyone was excited because I really had hit the stumps. I couldn't believe it! I don't know if they used that "take" or whether they cut from my run-up to somebody else hitting the wicket but I had to do it a few more times and, inevitably, I never hit the stumps again. It was a total fluke. But it was my moment of glory.'

ANNA AND JULIA'S FINEST HOUR – THE CHAMBERS CRICKET MATCH.

OLIVER FORD DAVIES

as Peter Foxcott

Oliver Ford Davies is no stranger to courtroom scenes. He played Lynn Redgrave's barrister in the BBC film Death of a Son, based on the true story of a woman who sought legal retribution after her son had inadvertently taken a drugs overdose, and he once suffered every man's nightmare – being prosecuted by Victor Meldrew.

'It was about 20 years ago,' recalls Oliver, 'in an episode of *Crown Court*. I played a miracle healer who had been held responsible for a woman's death. The widowed husband had been going around saying I was a charlatan, so I had to bring an action against him to clear my name. So in actual fact, I was the plaintiff. Richard Wilson was playing the opposing counsel and at the beginning of the week in rehearsal, he said to me: "This script is so weighted towards you, you're bound to get off." But by the end of the week, without altering any of the lines, Richard had so manipulated the jury with the words he'd been given that I was found guilty! The jury, which was always composed of 11 members of the public and one actor, didn't find for the plaintiff, so I lost the case. I've always held that against Richard Wilson...

“the jury were split 6-6, and I began to sweat at this. I thought, why on earth am I sweating? This is only fiction!”

'I remember at one point in the proceedings the jury were split 6-6, and I began to sweat at this. I thought, why on earth am I sweating? This is only fiction! Eventually the assistant producer went in to the jury room and said: "Look, you've got to make up your minds." And unfortunately for me, they did.'

Peter Foxcott QC, Head of Chambers at River Court, is in his late fifties, a big untidy bear of a man with a large voice. Although his work has provided ample experience of humanity, he is curiously unworldly, rather like judges who have never heard of Madonna. He is apt to accept the advice of like-minded peers rather than colleagues of greater ability

THE CHANCE TO GIVE KAVANAGH OUT LBW IS A PRAYER ANSWERED FOR UMPIRE PETER FOXCOTT.

and imagination, like Kavanagh, whose superior qualities he nevertheless acknowledges.

'Foxcott is the public school, Cambridge-educated establishment barrister,' says Oliver, 'so he's pitted against Kavanagh who comes from a lower middle-class background and has worked his way up. Although Foxcott is Head of Chambers, technically Kavanagh is a year senior to him – I think he "took silk" a year earlier. So if Kavanagh had wanted, he could have been Head of Chambers. But Kavanagh couldn't be bothered with the extra administrative hassle. Even so, Foxcott is very conscious that Kavanagh has the seniority and also that, if it came to the crunch, most people in chambers would listen to Kavanagh rather than him. So he tends to need to have Kavanagh on his side even though Kavanagh's views are far more liberal than his.

FOXCOTT IS VERY MUCH A BARRISTER OF THE OLD SCHOOL.

'Together with Aldermarten, Foxcott represents the right-wing of chambers although Aldermarten is probably even more to the right than Foxcott. Foxcott likes Aldermarten, wants his support and shares many of his views but he does have a slightly detached, ironic eye with regard to Aldermarten. He can see through him – but then again, most people can see through Aldermarten.

'Foxcott is a man with doubts about his own ability. In the first series, he remarked to Kavanagh: "I've always been a tortoise to your hare." He doesn't have spark; he's not inspired. He makes up for this by being a dogged, hard-worker although I suspect he likes to take on the easier cases that make money. I don't think the challenge is still there for him. He feels that he's given too much of his life to a routine profession, as a lot of people do at his age. They suddenly realise there's a world elsewhere and begin to think what they might have done with their lives. There have been suggestions that he might become a judge but that would mean a drop in salary. Foxcott probably earns around £250,000 a year and it's very hard to give that up. And I don't think Eleanor, his wife, would be prepared to sacrifice that.

'The Foxcotts have a big house in the country and he has a flat in town. What we don't know yet is whether he has a mistress. I think it would be fun if he did, particularly if she suddenly turned up in chambers, but I haven't yet managed to persuade Chris Kelly of the virtues. But I'm firmly rooting for Foxcott to have a mistress!'

Oliver Ford Davies has been hooked on acting since he was 15. 'I was brought up in Ealing and my father was a schoolteacher and keen amateur actor. I did a lot of school plays and in 1962 I was president of the Oxford University Dramatic Society. I played Othello and Falstaff – two of the big "heavies".

'Those were exciting days at Oxford. My contemporaries in the Dramatic Society included Dennis Potter and Alan Bennett, and it was also the time of Beyond the Fringe. In fact, I was in a production of *Bartholomew Fair* at Oxford with Dudley Moore and also Ken Loach. I remember Dudley did the music for it too. It's funny looking back: you just can't tell how people's careers will turn out. For example, the best student actress I was with at Oxford didn't go into the theatre at all – she became a teacher.'

Having gained a degree in History, Oliver landed a post as a history lecturer at Edinburgh University. 'But after only about three weeks in the job, I thought to myself: This isn't what I want to do with my life. I realised I wanted to act. I was lucky. I received a lot of support from the professor who said: "If you're going to do it, go now. Don't wait until you're 30 and have got a mortgage and a family. You probably won't have the courage then." So I took up acting professionally.'

“Foxcott is a man with doubts about his own ability”

The move has certainly paid dividends. From early parts at Birmingham Repertory Theatre, Oliver has progressed to become one of our busiest actors. He has enjoyed seasons with the Royal Shakespeare Company and the National Theatre, where he earned considerable praise as the Reverend Lionel Espy in David Hare's *Racing Demon*, while his many television credits include *Tenko, A Very Peculiar Practice, A Very British Coup, The Cloning of Joanna May* and *Between the Lines*.

'I think I got the part of Foxcott because I have worked so frequently with John Thaw. In fact, I've often ended up playing his sidekick in various productions. I was in *Mitch* with him and, in 1983, John did a season at the RSC. He was Cardinal Wolsey in *Henry VIII* and I played his secretary. I also did an *Inspector Morse* story called 'Second Time Around', in which I played a man who might have killed a girl 15 years previously and who was now suspected of another murder. Things looked so bad that he tried to kill himself in prison but eventually Morse proved his innocence. Then John and I were in David Hare's *Absence of War*. I played John's political adviser. We did 100 performances at the National and then did the TV version. Chris Kelly came to see John in the stage production of *Absence of War* and I was interviewed for Foxcott as a result of that. Since Kavanagh and Foxcott are supposed to have known each other for 20 years, it does help that John and I have worked together so much.

ALDERMARTEN LIKES TO KEEP ON THE RIGHT SIDE OF FOXCOTT.

'I had no shortage of research material for the role. I have a number of friends who are barristers and one who's a judge. He said: "I'm at Harrow all next week. Come and hear me do some judging." So I did the rounds of the courts there – you can't beat getting technical advice from the top!'

NICHOLAS JONES

as Jeremy Aldermarten

As barrister Jeremy Aldermarten, Nicholas Jones is used to giving people a hard time. But the boot was on the other foot when Nicholas found himself in court seven years ago.

'It still rankles to this day,' says Nicholas with feeling. 'I had to appear in court for not displaying a tax disc. I had already sent off for it but, as far as the magistrates were concerned, that didn't matter.

'They just said: "Were you, or were you not, displaying a tax disc?" I said: "But..."

'And they repeated the question. "Were you, or were you not, displaying a tax disc?"

'"But I'd sent off for it..."

'"Please answer the question. Were you, or were you not, displaying a tax disc?"

'"No, I wasn't."

'"Guilty."

'So I said: "To whom should I address this issue when clearly I just left my car on the street – I wasn't driving it – and I was waiting for my taxi to return?"

'They replied solemnly: "We are just here to respond to the legal situation."

'So you realise that the law is a complete ass and they don't like people being formal with them. I'm still angry now. Perhaps Aldermarten is my revenge on the legal profession...'

Jeremy Aldermarten is in his mid-forties. He is not exactly a sensitive soul and might have difficulty even in recognising that species. He enjoys the politics of chambers and has the ear of Foxcott who often refers to him for a second opinion. In return, Aldermarten tells him what he wants to hear. It would be easy, indeed tempting, to underestimate Aldermarten but, in a world still largely the preserve of the establishment, it could be a mistake. He is not without connections: nor is he without the single-mindedness to use them ruthlessly. Kavanagh is capable of outwitting him, but few others in chambers would attempt it. Aldermarten is besotted with Julia who, because of the power she has over him, can get away with treating him like an arrested adolescent – which, in essence, is what he is.

JEREMY ALDERMARTEN, A MAN OF MANY TALENTS, MOSTLY HIDDEN.

'Aldermarten is politically incorrect,' says Nicholas. 'which I think is one of the reasons

why he's such a popular character. He says things which people often feel in their hearts but which, in the current climate, are forbidden. Nobody is allowed to have these thoughts, let alone express them. But he just speaks his mind and I think that's very refreshing.

'He's very open – you know where you are with him. It's people who aren't what they say they are that are hard to deal with. And he's an innocent, which makes him susceptible. However, I suspect he's a very good lawyer.

'He's extremely selfish, and there's a tradition that goes back to Chekhov where characters are so selfish that it's funny. That's where the comedy lies – in absolute seriousness about himself. And make no mistake, he does takes himself very seriously.

'My only problem with Aldermarten was in finding the right clothes for him. I was told by our legal adviser, David Bradly, that the clothes I wanted were unacceptable, that Aldermarten would have been teased, frowned upon and considered rather vulgar for wearing them. Chambers is a very formalised world. So I reached a compromise with David and got myself the most vividly tasteful pair of braces I could find and took my jacket off. They're Pierre Cardin braces – very colourful and very expensive – and they're perfect. I was able to make my statement without intruding into the areas of poor taste. Aldermarten does wear some very sharp clothes. His suits definitely veer towards the continental – he's a sort of trans-Manche dresser.'

“Aldermarten is politically incorrect, which I think is one of the reasons why he's such a popular character”

The son of Royal Shakespeare Company actor Griffith Jones and sister of actress Gemma Jones (star of *The Duchess of Duke Street*), it was perhaps inevitable that Nicholas should pursue a career in the theatre. 'Dad has been in the business since 1930,' says Nicholas proudly, 'and has been at the RSC for 21 years. He's 85 now. So coming from a theatrical background does help the ease with which you can move into that world.'

Educated at Westminster School, Nicholas trained at RADA and the Bristol Old Vic, where he won the Gold Award. Prior to that, he had been a stage manager at Liverpool. 'My acting debut was at Liverpool in *Richard III*. I played a murderer and got knocked down a flight of steps by Richard.'

Since then, Nicholas has appeared in numerous productions, including *Major Barbara, Wild Honey* and *She Stoops to Conquer* at the National Theatre; films such as *Black Beauty* and *Cromwell*; and television series like *Wings*, in which he played a young fighter pilot, *The Flame Trees of Thika, The Price, Not a Penny More, Not a Penny Less*, Dennis Potter's *Lipstick On Your Collar, Sharpe's Company, Bramwell* and *A Touch of Frost*.

'Oddly enough, I've never worked with my sister. We were offered a TV series about a brother and sister years ago, but she said no, probably because she didn't like the idea of working with me although I've never asked her why she turned it down. A bit of sibling rivalry there, perhaps? Who knows?

'And I've only ever played a lawyer once before and that was in a remake of *King and*

Country. I played the Dirk Bogarde role alongside Michael Elphick. I was a prosecutor in that and I remember I had this huge two-page speech. There's a definite technique to it – you have to be able to hold a parenthesis as a barrister! They say that if you want to make yourself clear, you tell someone what you're going to say, then you say it, then you tell them what you've just said. And you've got to wrap that up in such a way that it doesn't sound as if you've been telling them it three times. Barristers call it man-management – I call it manipulation.'

As can be gathered, Nicholas has no great love for the legal profession. 'Maybe it stems back to my youth. It was mum and dad's hobby for a while to go to the Old Bailey and catch famous trials. I went once or twice and I remember the atmosphere in court being horrendous. I didn't like it at all. As a result, there was never the remotest chance of my wanting to become a lawyer.'

ALDERMARTEN'S INFATUATION WITH LUCY CARTWRIGHT (LESLEY MANVILLE) IS NOT THE FIRST TIME HE HAS MADE A FOOL OF HIMSELF OVER A WOMAN.

Cliff Parisi

as Tom Buckley

Cliff Parisi has been known to suffer for his art. In his early days as a stand-up comic, he and his partner, Andy Lindon, played some of the roughest pubs in London...

CLIFF PARISI AS SENIOR CLERK TOM BUCKLEY – THE POWER BEHIND THE THRONE.

The sort of places where the pool table is bolted to the floor lest it be used as an offensive weapon and the guard dogs wear shin pads. One night, Cliff and Andy's act went down so well that one of the audience pulled a knife on them!

'We called ourselves The Port Stanley Amateur Dramatic Society,' recalls Cliff, 'and we played a couple of Argentinian concert party comedians, predominantly taking the mickey out of the English. This was not long after the Falklands conflict so, in some places, it was still a bit of a sensitive subject. In one pub, a knife was pulled on us by somebody very patriotic who thought we were being unpatriotic. We decided not to hang around and argue.

'We did the routine for about a year. We performed at the Comedy Store as well as these dodgy pubs with about three people in the audience. We got into loads of nasty scrapes. The thing was you could never predict who was going to like you and who wasn't. Sometimes it was middle-class wallies, sometimes lefties and other times right-wingers. We didn't have an agent but, once we were established and people got to know about us, they'd phone us up and book us. But we soon learned which places to cross off our list.

“I remember the time we were pelted with tin cans by 300 kids in Tottenham”

'I remember the time we were pelted with tin cans by 300 kids in Tottenham – but apparently that was actually a sign of appreciation!'

Cliff was brought up in north London and first acquired the acting bug after playing the lead in a small film called *Piggy in the Middle* at the age of 14. 'I loved acting – it was one of the few things I could do but when I left school that same year, I drifted into all manner of odd jobs. I worked in office removals; I dug roads; later I was a mini cab driver; and, when I was 18, I worked in a disco in Spain on roller skates. I used to be dragged

PROPERTY NOTICES
PROPERTY NOTICES

through the streets on these skates. I also had a market stall in London where I sold dresses. I can still do the patter. It's a bit like acting in a way – you have to grab an audience and then keep them. I did that for one season but then I went bust. I'd sold my motorbike and my car to set it up but then had to lay out quite a lot of money to get a flat because I'd got a baby daughter.'

Undeterred, Cliff renewed his acting ambitions. 'I desperately needed an Equity card but knew that the only way I'd get one was through variety. So when I met Andy Lindon at an acting workshop I was attending in the evenings, we got together and formed our comedy double act. After doing that, I wanted to move into straight acting which first meant shaking off the stigma of being a comedian. It's very hard to be a comedian at the same time as being considered a serious actor. So I went into fringe theatre and some of the contacts, whom I had made through the theatre, moved into television and they took Andy and me with them.

'Even though we'd finished the double act (Andy still does a stand-up routine), we tended to get cast a lot together as actors, particularly at first, because we look quite funny as a pair. In a Central TV series called *Tales of Sherwood*, I was a cop and he was a villain. We were both in *Chancer* together and we did a play called *Dirty Dishes* which later became a TV film, in which I was a Colombian drug addict and he was an illegal immigrant.

UPSET OVER HIS WIFE'S DEPRESSION, BUCKLEY CAUSES A SCENE AT A BARRISTERS' GET-TOGETHER.

Cliff has since appeared in drama series such as *The Bill*, *Gone to the Dogs*, *Gone to Seed*, *Boon* and *The Darling Buds of May* as well as in sketch shows with Harry Enfield, Paul Merton, Fry and Laurie, Sean Hughes and the *KYTV* team.

'I still do the odd sketch in comedy shows if they're funny but more recently I've been doing straighter stuff which is nice. I really enjoyed playing Micky Wright in two series of *London's Burning*. He was a terrific character – he was a protagonist from a rival station, Borough. I only went out on one "shout" but it was brilliant, flying round the streets in a fire engine with the lights blazing and the sirens going – it's every kid's dream. It was a shame I couldn't do the last series but by then I was playing Daniel, the hospital porter, in *Bramwell*.'

And of course Cliff had also been signed up to play senior clerk Tom Buckley in *Kavanagh Q.C.* Tom Buckley is very quick-witted and has the ability to retain simultaneously dozens of pieces of information relating to widely differing cases and negotiations. He has little formal education, and hardly any detailed knowledge of the Law, but he has formidable intelligence and is an excellent, intuitive judge of people. Tough and forthright, he fears no-one in chambers, although he has a particular respect for his 'silks' because he knows them to be thorough-going professionals as well as good earners.

Kavanagh is the barrister to whom he feels closest and the two have a relationship of mutual regard, enjoying each other's sense of humour. On the whole, Tom is not a fan of women in chambers, but for Julia he is prepared to make a grudging exception. Tom likes a good drink when the work's done but, during office hours, he drives his staff hard. However they know that, as long as they do the business, he will be a loyal ally.

“Tom is not a fan of women in chambers, but for Julia he is prepared to make a grudging exception”

Curiously, Tom Buckley is not the first time Cliff has played a senior clerk on television. 'In *The Guilty*, I played a senior clerk called Cliffy! Tom's a bit older than Cliffy. He's in his early forties, he's got four kids but his wife has been suffering from post-natal depression.

'I researched the world of senior clerks for both *The Guilty* and *Kavanagh Q.C.* I've got no legal background at all although an uncle of mine was a prison officer. But he was the black sheep of the family!

'Clerks are very rich and very working-class. The job is usually hereditary – it's passed down among the family. They work hard and play hard. At the end of the day, they like a bottle of champagne – they're good drinkers. They're good at their job; they think on their feet and make decisions very quickly. And they've got incredible memories. Yet they're pretty guarded about what they do. I think they thought I was going to come along and expose all their practices on TV, so they kept some things secret from me – like how they manage to get their own way and get cases set for certain dates when it suits them. They've got these tricks of the trade which they like to keep to themselves.

'There are certain routines you have to know though such as the way they rotate the barristers and how they allocate the work. And I got to learn about the basic running of the office – what the different coloured bits of paper mean. And they've got a language all of their own with plenty of jargon. It's a quickfire code, paraphrased to make everything very quick, very brief.

'Senior clerks really are the engine of the whole of chambers. They carry a lot of responsibility on their shoulders and it definitely doesn't pay for a barrister to cross them. I heard about one senior clerk who sent a barrister all over the country on ridiculous cases, such as parking fines, just because he didn't like him. It cost the barrister more in fares than he ever made out of the cases. He was sent to the bleakest places imaginable in the middle of winter, keeping him miles away from home for four or five days at a time. The senior clerks call it “running for your money”.'

At the same time as he was filming the second series of Kavanagh, Cliff was also working on the second run of *Bramwell*. 'I'm happy to be doing two great series and to be a jobbing actor. There's less pressure and responsibility on you that way. It's nice working with people like Harry Enfield and Paul Merton but I don't really envy them. I'm happy to be in everything and not be noticed. Besides, I'm not very good with money. So it's probably just as well I'm not a senior clerk either...'

LIKE MANY OF HIS BRETHREN, BUCKLEY IS NOT AVERSE TO THE ODD GLASS OF BUBBLY.

JENNY JULES

as Alex Wilson

Jenny Jules was left in something of a dilemma when first interviewed for the part of Alex Wilson in Kavanagh Q.C.

'It was three days before I was due to move out to the US for six months to join my actor husband, Ralph Brown, who was working out there. I was going to stay out there and see what happened work-wise. But when they offered me *Kavanagh*, I was put in a quandary. I didn't want to turn it down but I knew Ralph would be disappointed at my not joining him. Fortunately since we're in the same profession, it was easier for him to understand...though it took him ages to forgive me! But we managed to deal with it and I flew over as often as I could.'

ALEX WILSON HAS RECENTLY QUALIFIED AS A JUNIOR BARRISTER.

Jenny traces her determination to succeed as an actress back to a childhood rejection.

'When I was six, they were choosing people for a school Christmas play. We were at assembly and everyone was putting their hands up, including my brother who's 20 months older than me. And they picked him to play one of the leading characters and totally ignored me. What made it worse was that the play was going to be performed on my birthday! I was furious.

'So I just became this jumped-up little supercow who wanted to perform for everybody,' laughs Jenny. 'Together with my young sisters and my best friend, who lived next door, I formed a little dance group. We sang and choreographed our routines, doing Abba stuff and the songs from *Bugsy Malone*. Then when I was 13, I studied modern ballet – but hated it. I used to cry because the discipline was so strict. But it didn't put me off acting and at 15, I joined a youth theatre. I was totally and utterly hooked. One of a family of seven (six girls and one boy), Jenny is by no means the only member of the Jules clan to have gone into show busi-

JENNY JULES SAYS ACTING IS HER FIRST LOVE.

ness. 'My brother John is in a band called Undercover. They got to Number Two in the charts a couple of years back with a version of "Baker Street". And one of my younger sisters, Lucy, is a singer – she went to the "Fame" school in Croydon.

'I don't know where we got this urge to perform from, because mum used to be an administrator with Marks & Spencer and dad was a mechanic. Mind you, we're a pretty diverse family. Of my other sisters, Mollie is a social worker; Dee is a housewife; Natasha has just done a law degree and wants to be a barrister; and Marilyn is a nun in the Caribbean!

'Certainly having a sister studying law came in handy for researching my role in Kavanagh. She would come along to court with me and the pair of us would sit there and soak it all up. Also, Ralph did a law degree before becoming an actor, so he has been able to help me; and a girlfriend of mine is a solicitor. So I'm surrounded by legal people.

'I also met a young black female barrister and we've since become good friends. She taught me a lot about the various difficulties Alex would have to face. A lot of "isms" exist in chambers and Alex has collected most of them. This barrister told me that the biggest "ism" Alex would have to deal would be sexism rather than racism. If you're cute, you can combat racism in chambers, but if you're a woman...

“ I don't know where we got this urge to perform from, because mum used to be an administrator with Marks & Spencer and dad was a mechanic ”

'She told me that it was the women who voted for the wigs to stay. If you're dressed in ordinary clothes, a client can call you "luv" or "babe", but, if you're in a wig or a gown, they have to show respect.'

The character Jenny played in the series, Alex Wilson, applied to River Court as plain A Wilson. Some of the more reactionary members of chambers received the shock of their lives when A Wilson turned out to be not only a woman but also a black woman into the bargain. Her intellectual ability was undeniable (she has a first class degree in Law from Cambridge) and, after a little gentle persuasion from Julia Piper, an old school friend of Alex's, Aldermarten agreed to use his influence to convince Foxcott of her merits. Thus she joined as Aldermarten's pupil. He soon took a shine to her, so much so that, in an amorous moment, he placed his hand on her leg in a wine bar. Alex was able to turn the incident to her own advantage and secure a tenancy. At times she has had to curb a natural tendency to say what she thinks but her forthright attitude has meant that she has more than held her own in chambers.

Jenny says: 'Although Alex is no longer a pupil – she's a junior barrister now – she's still feisty with lots of inner strength. In that environment, you have to learn to protect yourself – it's the only way to survive.'

Jenny has been acting professionally for 10 years. 'When I was 16 and still at school, I played an extra in *The Great White Hope* at the Tricycle Theatre, Kilburn. And a year later, I was offered my Equity card to do *The Black Jacobins* with Norman Beaton. I was supposed to play Norman's wife in the prologue which was a little unlikely since she was about 50 and I was only 17. I was so slight I had to be padded out with cushions but what really did it was my high-pitched voice. I couldn't control it, so in the end they cut my speech from the prologue and I just walked on with Norman.

'I side-stepped university to get my Equity card but I think I will go to university at some time in the future even if I spend a year there and decide I know more than the tutor.'

After *The Black Jacobins*, Jenny worked non-stop for four years. Her television credits include *Desmonds, Little Napoleons* and *Prime Suspect II*, her first brush with the law. 'I played law student Sarah Allen, whose brother was the baddie, and at the end of the story, I had this big ten-page denouement with Helen Mirren. She's fabulous – we had such a laugh together.'

Everything is looking rosy for Jenny who is currently the only woman in the cast of *Two Trains Running* at the Tricycle Theatre. 'Mum and Dad are really proud of us all. And they love Kavanagh, especially because John Thaw's in it. In fact, things are going so well that I've almost forgiven my brother for beating me to that part in the school play all those years ago. But not quite...'

ALEX'S CONFIDENCE CAN SOMETIMES BE MISTAKEN FOR ARROGANCE.

Daisy Bates

as Kate Kavanagh

Daisy Bates' television debut was less than auspicious. As a baby, she was due to appear in an episode of Poldark which starred her late father Ralph as the villainous George Warleggan.

'But I was sacked for screaming the place down because the director had a beard. I just didn't like beards.'

With Ralph Bates as a dad and former model Virginia Wetherall for a mum, Daisy was born into a show business family. 'I'm told my first steps were to Robin Ellis, who played Ross Poldark, because I was so used to seeing him in the house.

'Throughout my childhood, I was surrounded by actors. But it was nothing out of the ordinary to me. As far as I was concerned, dad was simply doing a job.

“I was sacked for screaming the place down because the director had a beard. I just didn't like beards”

'I soon started acting in school plays. At four, I was an angel in a nativity and, at nine, I played Fairy Stumblebum's assistant in *Cinderella*. I remember I had to sing which was not my strong point. I was principally a dancer. I think they only picked me because I was short, sweet and angelic!

'I trained as a ballet dancer till I was 16, so I had the big theatrical discipline, training for five hours every day. Mum and dad never encouraged me to become an actress because they knew the pros and cons of it, but I did appear in three series of *Forever Green* as Freddy, the daughter of John Alderton and Pauline Collins. John and Pauline were great mates of mum and dad, so that's how I got the part. And dad knew that they would look after me.

KATE KAVANAGH – THE PROBLEM CHILD OF THE FAMILY.

'As a result of *Forever Green*, I got an agent and that led to other work. But it was always done in my school holidays, so that it never conflicted with my studies. That was the deal. It was like having a holiday job. Some people do a paper round – I went off and did a TV series.

'I think dad was rather shocked when I took up acting. He felt it was really important for me to keep up my studies. He was very bright and went to university, and he wanted me to do the same. He used to say that one day he'd get a proper job – be a doctor or something.'

Daisy went to Charterhouse School to do her 'A' Levels – and appeared in a production of *The Crucible* – but her world was shattered when her dad, fresh from his success in *Dear John*, died from pancreatic cancer at the age of 51. Daisy was 17 at the time.

By then, Daisy had begun to consider a career in law. 'I went off to India and Paris and then to St. Andrew's University to study theology. The intention was that I'd get my degree and then switch to a law conversion course. But I'd only been at university for a term when it all slotted into place. I dropped out, thinking that maybe it wasn't for me and that I wanted to get back into acting. And then I got Kavanagh. The timing was perfect.

KATE USED LUKE TO ESTABLISH GROUND RULES WITH HER PARENTS.

'Kate Kavanagh is the problem child of the pair,' says Daisy who, at 21, is three years older than her screen character. 'She's a bit of a headache for her parents. She's very headstrong and a mixture of them both, which makes her pretty difficult at times.

'But she is a sensible girl. In the first series, she wanted to sleep with her boyfriend Luke. She kept trying to get permission from her parents but couldn't win her father round to the idea. And when she did eventually elicit a degree of approval, she decided against it. She was simply testing them, laying down the principles. And in this series, she has a relationship with her university tutor which needless to say doesn't go down too well with James and Lizzie. But although she goes off the rails occasionally, she's intelligent and can handle it.'

Daisy was thrilled to land the part of Kate and knows that her dad would have been equally pleased for her. 'He would have been really proud and delighted that I'd been given the opportunity to learn from such a professional as John Thaw.

'Mum and my 18-year-old brother Will were really happy for me too. Mum has been incredibly supportive, even when I quit university, and they were both swigging champagne while they watched the first episode. Poor Will has dutifully listened to me learning my lines.

'Dad used to do that when I was in *Forever Green*. One time I'd been going through a particular scene and he just looked at me and said: "God, Daisy, you did that really well." That bit of praise was so important, to know that he believed in me, and I'll always cherish it.'

For Daisy, one of the most rewarding aspects of doing *Kavanagh Q.C.* has been hearing so many people remembering her father with such warmth and affection. 'The make-up people worked with him, as did Oliver Ford Davies. Over 20 years ago, they did

WHILE AWAY AT CAMBRIDGE, KATE STUNS THE FAMILY BY HAVING AN AFFAIR WITH HER MARRIED TUTOR.

a play together with Mia Farrow called *Mary Rose*. One day on set, Oliver brought in some cuttings and told me all the stories about making the play. It was really nice.

'That's what I like about television – it's like a family. Even the driver, Chris Streeter, who picked me up each morning, was the same one who used to collect me on *Forever Green*. And he used to drive my dad. So it's like having an uncle.

'I'm still interested in law. A mate of mine is studying it – his father's a lawyer – and I find it a fascinating world. I remember when I was 14, trailing a barrister for a day. But I've decided that acting's the career for me now.

'And what's made *Kavanagh* all the more enjoyable is that none of the directors have had beards.'

But surely Daisy wouldn't scream at them now?

'I might...'

TOM BRODIE

as Matt Kavanagh

Life is hectic for 17-year-old Tom Brodie. Over the past year, he has been a regular in two succesful drama series, as well as playing comedian Paul Merton as a boy.

'I was young Paul in Paul Merton's *World of Comedy*,' explains Tom. 'I must have been chosen because I look a bit like him, or at least like he did back in the Seventies. It was great fun to do because I had to wear all these crazy clothes – flares, tank tops and tight jeans. It was like a journey through fashion hell. And to top it off, I sometimes had to wear this wig with awful sideburns.

'I love Paul Merton in *Have I Got News For You?* and I've got all his videos, so it was quite funny actually working with him. You see people on the telly but, when you start working with them, they're just colleagues. For the first day you think, "Oh my God, it's him" but after that you start respecting them for what nice people they are. It's the same with John Thaw in *Kavanagh*.'

"I've been so busy that I've had to postpone taking my "A" Levels"

Besides playing Matt Kavanagh, Tom is also vet's son Steven Holt in the BBC series *The Vet*, set in rural Devon. 'I seem to be cornering the market in sons,' says Tom without a hint of irony.

'I was doing *The Vet* and *Kavanagh Q.C.* simultaneously. Fortunately, the respective production teams managed to liaise, so that I didn't have to be in two places at the same time. That could have been a bit of a problem.

MATT KAVANAGH – A PRETTY STRAIGHTFORWARD GUY ACCORDING TO TOM BRODIE WHO PLAYS HIM ON SCREEN.

'I've been so busy that I've had to postpone taking my "A" levels. There's no way I could have done everything. I did the first half of the course and I may do the rest this year. When I was doing the first series of Kavanagh, I was also revising for my GCSEs. So in any breaks, I had my head in a book, worrying about my exams. As it turned out, I needn't have worried too much because I managed to get eight GCSEs.'

Tom, who attends George Abbott School in his native Guildford, kept Kavanagh a secret from most of his classmates. 'I just told them I was working and left it at that, but

obviously my close friends wanted to know why I hadn't been at school for two months!'

Tom says he fell into acting. 'My mum and dad are both teachers, though fortunately not at my school. I think I'd have got a lot of flak from the other kids if they had been. When I was 10, my mum saw an ad in the local paper for auditions for a production of *Treasure Island* at the Redgrave Theatre, Farnborough. She said, "Why don't we go along?" So I went to the auditions for a laugh. I ended up playing Jim Hawkins and they said, "Get yourself an agent", which I did.

'After that, I did two series of a children's sci-fi programme, *Watt On Earth*, then *Streetwise* and two series of *Criss Cross* in which I played Mookie. For that, I had a pudding bowl haircut and little round glasses. Even my family were hard pushed to recognise me.

'Working on *Kavanagh* was different. I had to be much more mature because there weren't loads of kids my own age to mess around with. It took me about a week to settle in and then I felt relaxed. Working with John Thaw has been absolutely brilliant – I've learned so much from him.'

MATT IS DISTINCTLY UNDERWHELMED BY HIS FATHER'S WORK.

Matt Kavanagh is heavily into computer games like other teenagers are into Ecstasy. He's intelligent but he hasn't yet realised his full potential at Westminster School. Lizzie and Kavanagh do their best to chivvy him along, although Lizzie knows better than her husband how to motivate him. Matt hardly gives a second thought to Kavanagh's work – as far as he's concerned, it simply provides him with a comfortable standard of living. In any case, among Matt's peers, barristers are bracketed with policemen and politicians as shady characters or self-seeking scumbags. What possesses grown men to wear wigs, they wonder? Treated as a lower sub-species by his sister, Matt wants to be Bob Marley when he grows up.

'Matt's pretty straightforward,' says Tom. 'His parents are a bit overworked so he doesn't get to see them as much as he'd like but his sister keeps his feet firmly on the ground. He was very image-conscious but he's getting out of that because now it's imagey not to be imagey! Apart from a bit more parental attention, the one thing he is definitely lacking is a regular girlfriend. I think he's gagging for a girlfriend...'

Tom, whose older sister Melissa is at university studying English, doesn't share the views of some young actors who later reflect that they have missed out on their youth. 'If I hadn't done acting, I might have got better grades in my exams, but on the other hand I've had such a good time.

'I love the camaraderie on filming – the practical jokes. If somebody's got a flashy new car and keeps going on about it, a couple of the crew will lift the bonnet and put in half a dozen kippers. So when that person turns the heater on, there's this terrible fishy smell.

CHAPTER SIX

Kavanagh on location

In his wig and gown, James Kavanagh looks every inch the smart barrister about town, light years away from the crumpled Rumpole.

But now the secret of Kavanagh's wig can be revealed. Before being placed on John Thaw's head, it has been dipped in coffee.

The person responsible for this seemingly curious behaviour is make-up supervisor Sarah Grundy, but she says there is a perfectly logical explanation for it. 'We buy our wigs new – at £345 a head – but, if you use them straight away, they tend to glow on screen because they absorb all the light. This makes it very difficult for the lighting cameraman. Added to which, very few barristers wear brand new wigs. So we speed up the ageing process by dipping them all in coffee – it makes them look nice and worn.

'Similarly, we age them around the front edge with dark eye-liner. It gives them that natural grubbiness. In fact, in chambers, there's great kudos attached to how old and tatty a wig is. Some are so old that, as they unravel, bits have begun to stick out, but we can't copy that too closely because it would be distracting in close-up. We hack into them a bit with scissors to make them look spiky but, overall, we do try to keep them reasonably neat. I like to give them slightly different colours though. For instance, worn by someone who smokes, a wig would be a bit yellow and we achieve that effect with coloured spray.

LAST MINUTE TOUCHING-UP TO KAVANAGH'S WIG.

'We buy the wigs from Ede and Ravenscroft in London's Chancery Lane – it was Ravenscroft who designed the very first barristers' wig. The wigs come in different sizes, like hats, and we've bought eight so far. We do occasionally have to hire additional wigs for big courtroom scenes. Just about the hardest thing is working

ANDY SERKIS IS MADE UP FOR 'THE BURNING DECK.'

A BLOOD-STAINED T-SHIRT FROM 'TRUE COMMITMENT.'

out who would wear a wig in court. For example, if it's a Crown Court, everyone in a black gown wears a wig but, if there's no jury, the clerk of the court doesn't wear one. It can be a bit of a nightmare.'

One of Sarah's most exacting tasks on *Kavanagh Q.C.* was creating the injuries suffered by David Lomax from the industrial accident in the episode 'A Stranger in the Family'. 'The victim had his head crushed, so for that we approached a neurosurgeon at St Mary's Teaching Hospital. They have plenty of relevant books plus slides of trauma cases and you just choose the ones you want and work from those. So the wounds you see on screen are based on real-life injuries. We just have to remember to tone them down for television.'

The biggest problem facing the make-up department last year was keeping the cast cool during the long hot summer. Make-up artist Margaret O'Keefe explains: 'We had to make them up in the morning, re-touch them throughout the day and, on really hot days, re-do them at lunch times. And, on top of that, there was a lot of mopping of brows. One of the hottest days came when we filmed the riot scene for 'True Commitment'. That was really hard work because everybody was getting sunburnt too. So we had to apply loads of sun block, especially on foreheads.

“The wounds you see on screen are based on real-life injuries”

'The sun also creates a continuity problem. Although we ask actors not to sit out and sunbathe – and they're very good about it – they might spend a weekend off in the garden and inadvertently get brown. In the previous scene, they might be pale, so we have to keep a watch for things like that, which means constantly taking Polaroids to monitor their tans.'

A real coup for Kavanagh was being given permission to film on the deck of Nelson's flagship, HMS Victory, for the episode 'The Burning Deck'. 'I must admit I was amazed at the tremendous co-operation we got from the Navy,' says Chris Kelly, 'since our court martial story certainly wasn't a plug for them. But we were able to go down to Portsmouth and not only film on Victory, which, in itself was a great privilege, but also reconstruct a fire exercise on HMS Cardiff. I think the Navy realised we would do the episode anyway, so they thought they might as well co-operate, so that it would be accurate.'

JOHN THAW CHATS TO NAVAL EXPERTS DURING A BREAK IN FILMING.

The episode was especially poignant for director Charles Beeson, whose father was commodore of Portsmouth's Nelson Dockyard some 10 years ago. Charles says: 'My parents lived in a dockyard residence and, although I had left home by then, I used to visit them there from time to time. So it was really strange going back there to film.

'The story is very much a balance between the old Navy and the new Navy, so being able to place it in a historic setting like Victory gave it extra strength. As Victory is such a major tourist attraction, we had to film early in the morning before she opened to the public at 10am. We had a 7am start. In our scene, naval officers were showing Kavanagh and fellow QC Eleanor Harker (played by Geraldine James) around the ship, saying you couldn't possibly come to Portsmouth and not see this. So Kavanagh and Harker were doing the tourist bit themselves. In fact, Victory is still a commissioned ship. The Captain insists she's still one of the flagships of the Navy. The fact that she's surrounded by concrete seems to have escaped his attention...

ALL OF THE CREW WERE PRIVILEGED TO BE ABLE TO FILM ON BOARD HMS VICTORY.

'Filming in the mess was particularly fascinating because we were on the site where Nelson was laid to rest after being brought back from the Battle of Trafalgar. He had been pickled in brandy for six weeks at sea to keep him in one piece! The Navy still has great reverence for Nelson. They've recently allowed a portrait of Emma Hamilton into the mess, which is quite a liberating move. She had previously been banished outside.

"He's a very special actor – incredibly supportive..."

'On HMS Cardiff, we shot in the engine room and down below. We were able to reproduce a fire practice using the ship's own fire-fighters – real crew members were allocated to help us. When we did the recce, and I was down in Portsmouth briefing the Navy on what we wanted to achieve, we were just leaving HMS Cardiff when a real fire started. It was only a small electrical fire in the engine room, but they thought it was a little ironic. I hasten to add it wasn't started by us!'

While the exteriors for the episode were shot in Portsmouth, the interiors were filmed elsewhere. Charles Beeson explains: 'We didn't have the budget to film the whole episode in Portsmouth, so we accurately copied what existed of Portsmouth in terms of court martial rooms and corridors, and recreated it at various other places. We shot the court scenes in the council chamber of Runnymede Borough Council's civic offices at Addlestone in Surrey. Our designer, Michael Pickwoad, did such a good job, not just in copying Portsmouth but in capturing the spirit of the place, that, when the naval officers came to see our set, they were so impressed that they wanted to trade it in for the real thing.'

Charles, who has recently worked on *Band of Gold*, also pays tribute to John Thaw. 'He's a very special actor – incredibly supportive and I learned a lot from him. My only

FOR DIRECTOR CHARLES BEESON (ABOVE), FILMING AT PORTSMOUTH WAS ESPECIALLY POIGNANT.

PORTSMOUTH PROVIDES A HIGHLY EFFECTIVE BACKDROP TO 'THE BURNING DECK.'

previous connection with the law was three weeks' jury service. I didn't think I was going to see much action because, after I had taken the oath, I had to stand down when the defence barrister objected to me. I spent the next four days sitting around feeling persecuted. By the time I was called again, I was really fed up and didn't want to give up any more of my time. So I tried to put on the same expression as before in the hope that I wouldn't get picked, but this time I was. I turned to the judge and said: "Look, I can't do this. I've got to go filming." He simply told me to sit down and get on with it. And in fact I ended up really enjoying it – it was just like a soap opera.'

The court martial scenes for 'The Burning Deck' were filmed at Addlestone in August when there were no committee meetings. Michael Pickwoad was struck by the building's uncanny resemblance to the court martial room on HMS Nelson. 'There were even the same sort of windows. You can achieve a military effect on a set simply by arranging everything in a neat and orderly manner, but dressing the building to look naval allowed me greater scope because it's impossible to overdo the symbolism with the Navy. For example, we hung ancient flags around the room and these provided a great sense of tradition which the Navy is full of. The flags weren't really old, so it was down to us to make them look like museum pieces. We bleached some, attacked others with wire brushes and I took a blowtorch to one to give it that effect of being riddled with bullet holes.

'The flags were good visually and they weren't blue. In court, all of the Navy stuff is very dark blue, which would look almost black on screen, so we used a lighter shade of blue. Even so, I still needed something to break it up – and the flags served the purpose admirably. We also borrowed a couple of genuine cannons from HMS Nelson. The Navy kindly brought them up from Portsmouth one day and took them back the next, when we had finished filming.

THE COURT MARTIAL SCENES WERE SHOT IN COUNCIL CHAMBERS AT ADDLESTONE.

'One thing that intrigued me when we were looking round the mess in Portsmouth was that, wherever there was a portrait of Nelson, there was a posy of flowers placed underneath. He still is God as far as the Navy is concerned. I decided to symbolise that for a scene where the officer admitted to being in love with one of the ratings. In the officer's room, I put a print of Nelson in one corner and one of Emma Hamilton over the bed. I hope someone will spot it and find it amusing. Another private joke is the list of commodores on the board of our fictional vessel, HMS Hawke. The names are those of the production unit jumbled up. We had to have someone's names, so we thought we might as well have ours!'

“The flags weren't really old, so it was down to us to make them look like museum pieces”

For costume designer Sue Yelland, getting the naval uniforms right frequently meant burning the midnight oil. 'The Navy loaned us most of the uniforms. They let us have officers' uniforms while the uniform equipment store let us use the "gash" – the stuff that they're going to throw away. But the problem was working out who wears what. Our technical adviser on the episode, Commander Blackett, was extremely helpful. He showed me the ropes and sent me books on naval uniforms. But, to be honest, I'm not even sure that the Navy is always 100 per cent sure itself. I remember him phoning me at about 10.30 one night to say that one of the officers shouldn't have a hook on the arm of his uniform – it had to come off. So I had to remove the hook and pray that it wasn't too visible on the shot we'd already done.

'Sewing all the bits and pieces on to the uniforms and taking off obsolete medals and adding new ones was a nightmare. I got most of the medals from the costume hire shop, Angel's and Berman's, and, on our first day of filming in Portsmouth, I plonked them down in front of Commander Blackett and said: "Now you award the medals according to their age, rank and so forth."'

"I decided it was best not to go into a shop and ask for half-a-dozen swastikas"

Sue is equally painstaking over the costumes for those in chambers. 'There are two or three good legal shops in London who supply all the clothes for the legal profession, so I get the costumes from them. But it is so essential to get it right and I find myself talking to the Head Usher's office at the Royal Courts of Justice to find out what a particular judge would wear in a certain situation. It is such a complicated set-up that sometimes even they are not sure.

'Dressing Kavanagh is considerably easier. John Thaw and I went shopping at the start of the first series and we bought some very smart Savile Row suits for Kavanagh. For the new series, I paid homage to clothes designer Jean Muir, who died a few days before we filmed the second episode. I went out and bought some Jean Muir suits and put Lisa Harrow in them. Lizzie's a bit more fashion-conscious than her husband. Kavanagh would wear the same raincoat for years.'

JOHN THAW WAITS PATIENTLY WHILE KAVANAGH'S ATTIRE IS ADJUSTED.

Sue's most unusual assignment was to dress the students and neo-Nazi demonstrators for the episode 'True Commitment'. 'It meant I had to obtain swastikas from somewhere. I had no intention of making my own, so I toured Carnaby Street and its environs. I decided it was best not to go into a shop and ask for half-a-dozen swastikas – I might have got some funny looks – so instead, I just cruised around and picked up what I wanted.

'A lot of the student clothes had to be ragged and tie-dyed with slogans on. That took me a whole weekend, sloshing things around over a dye bar. And for the character, who got knifed, I had to provide three identical outfits – one before the stabbing, one during and one after.'

But Sue is no stranger to seeking out the bizarre. 'I remember I had to dress a crucifixion scene for American TV. With Jesus and assorted thieves needing to be up on crosses, I cleaned Soho out of posing pouches in one night!'

The demonstration and subsequent riot for 'True Commitment' were filmed in Chiswick, after two other London boroughs had expressed reservations about allowing such a sensitive subject to be tackled on their streets. Assistant location manager Pat

Karam says: 'Merton refused to let us film because of the racist content and Greenwich said they weren't at all keen – they didn't want our demonstration to act as a catalyst. But Hounslow Council has its own film officer and he was able to smooth the way for us to film in Chiswick.

'We filmed the scene with 150 extras, police vans and a police horse all day one Friday. Obviously the residents had been told in advance, as had the police. Thanks to the police, we were able to shut off a T-junction just off Chiswick High Road and set up a diversion system, so that there wasn't a constant stream of cars interrupting the filming. It was no great inconvenience to motorists – it only added something like 30 seconds to their journey times.

'We didn't get any complaints from residents. They spent most of the day watching us and seemed to think it all rather festive...though I'm not sure they'd want it to happen on their doorsteps every week.'

AROUND 150 EXTRAS ASSEMBLE FOR THE DEMONSTRATION IN 'TRUE COMMITMENT.'

THE QUIET STREETS OF CHISWICK ARE TURNED INTO A BATTLEGROUND, ALL FOR THE BENEFIT OF THE CAMERAS.

A regular filming location is Kavanagh's house overlooking Wandsworth Common. Location manager David Kennaway found it through a company called Lavish Locations, which specialises in hiring out homes to film companies. 'The house is owned by a builder,' says David, 'and we usually film there for two days at a time. When we're there, the family invariably take off for the day.'

The house is ideal for designer Michael Pickwoad because it needs very little alteration for television. 'It's a very smart house,' says Michael, 'and a lot of the furniture is just right for the Kavanaghs. We do change some items, if they're in the way, or if they're too big or too small, or if they don't quite work visually. We also play around with the bedhead and curtains in the Kavanaghs' bedroom. The existing ones don't quite match, which doesn't matter a jot in real life, but on television it can jar. When you see things framed, as you do on TV, you think: "Why have they put that there?" Seeing a house on screen is not like being in a real house – on TV, you only see what you're shown.'

New Court in Middle Temple serves as the exterior for River Court Chambers but the courtroom interiors are scattered far and wide. 'Each episode has one major trial and sometimes a minor one,' says Michael Pickwoad, 'so we use a lot of courtrooms. That's our biggest challenge, finding somewhere to film the court scenes. And not only can't you film in Crown courts, you're not even allowed to take photographs in them, which makes it very difficult for me to recreate the interiors elsewhere. I have to go in and have eyes like Instamatics! So when I visited the courts in the Strand prior to converting Chiswick Town Hall into a High court, I had to look and remember as well as make sketches of details like the coat of arms.

CAPTURING THE ACTION AS THE DEMONSTRATION BECOMES A RIOT.

'The courtroom in 'Men of Substance' was based on Woolwich Court. We recreated it at the University of Hertfordshire's conference centre at Hatfield, which has a similar modern, hi-tech feel to Woolwich. We were allowed in to Woolwich one morning before they sat, so that we could measure up and take notes. As courtrooms go, it was not unattractive with nicely co-ordinated colours. Because Woolwich deals with a lot of high-security terrorist and drugs cases, the jury are situated out of sight beneath the gallery, so that they can't be nobbled by anybody looking down from above. I was able to sit in the gallery and soak up the atmosphere, but we weren't allowed to see the special security door through which the prisoners emerge into court. So we simulated our own door, which we opened by pressing a series of buttons – a bit like something from a James Bond movie. Director Charles

PRODUCER CHRIS KELLY (LEFT) AND DIRECTOR ANDREW GRIEVE (RIGHT) ON LOCATION.

Beeson decided to shoot that sequence through a video camera to relay to the audience the idea of a heavy security presence.

'The court we had used for the previous episode was an old-fashioned one at Stratford, East London, and was much more people's idea of a typical courtroom. The two together made a good contrast.

'The central plot to 'Men of Substance' was that drugs were being smuggled into the country inside carcasses of contaminated meat. We were originally going to use beef but then we thought about switching to pork. We had a few misgivings because pork is less acceptable to certain sections of the community but in the end we had no choice, partly because of the cost – sides of beef are incredibly expensive – but also because pork would be easier to manage. The carcass of a cow would have weighed so much that we wouldn't have been able to move it.'

Getting items such as 20 sides of pork from a wholesaler falls to production buyer Jeanne Vertigan and her assistant Jo Barrs. 'That was pretty straightforward,' says Jeanne. 'The wholesaler simply took them back afterwards. Often the hardest things to find are those which should be the simplest, like very boring, government-issue furniture, because everyone throws it away. For our court martial scenes, we needed a room full of extremely ordinary chairs. We tried hire companies, auctions, second-hand dealers – all without success – and in the end we had to borrow some from the Home Office. But we were completely stumped by one requirement for the same episode – busts of admirals. We actually found a couple in the Naval Museum but unfortunately they wouldn't allow them to be released.'

Over the years, director of photography Nigel Walters has become something of an expert in courtroom dramas, having worked on such productions as *Death of a Son* and a Russian period piece, *The Kremlin Farewell*. 'I suppose my style is ideal for courtrooms because I don't put in extra lighting which means the room doesn't get too hot. And when actors are in there for seven or eight days at a time – as they are on Kavanagh – it can get pretty stifling.

'I work closely with the director, and my job is to interpret his wishes while maintaining a certain style and standard. On a daily basis, I have to ensure continuity, that things are of the right mood in relation to the script, and that we have the highest standard of cinematography.

“The helicopter developed a fault, and we ended up having to make an emergency landing on the Isle of Wight”

'Sunlight is a cinematographer's greatest enemy,' says Nigel, who worked with John Thaw on *A Year In Provence* and, nearly 20 years ago, with Nicholas Jones when he played a young flying officer in *Wings*. 'Sunlight is very harsh, not at all flattering, so I'm looking to control it, maybe by blocking it out. One of the problems with filming in summer is that the script may call for evening or night, but there isn't any darkness – at least not within working hours. You can do night-time interiors during the day, simply by drawing the curtains. You can make sunlight look like moonlight. The sun and the moon do exactly the same thing – it's just that one is more intense than the other. If you reduce the intensity of the sun with a filter, it can easily pass as the moon. What you can't disguise in such situations is the sky, so you have to keep that out of shot.

'I always try to use light to the best dramatic effect. For example, I find that if you shoot against a window, it's usually more dramatic than if you shoot with the window behind you, because the light is not so flat or boring. Sometimes you need to create light. You can convey the passage of time through artificial lighting. Different angles of light coming into a room suggest the sun at different times of day. And you can make scenes look warmer or colder by adding filters. But, on night shoots, you have to be careful that the light doesn't look too artificial. It's all a question of achieving the right balance.'

As yet, *Kavanagh Q.C.* has only ventured out of Britain once. And that was just for a day's filming in Strasbourg with Lisa Harrow. Chris Kelly says: 'Although it was expensive, it was probably easier to get to Strasbourg than to Glasgow.

'But we did take to the air in the first series to film Kavanagh's yacht off the Isle of

JOHN THAW IN CONSULTATION WITH DIRECTOR ANDREW GRIEVE.

Wight. We hired this magnificent yacht and I was up in the helicopter which was doing all the aerial shots. But then something happened which definitely wasn't in the script. The helicopter developed a fault, and we ended up having to make an emergency landing on the Isle of Wight. Nobody likes emergencies in a helicopter, or indeed anywhere else where you haven't got control of the wheel. So all in all, it was pretty hairy.'

Chapter Seven

Kavanagh's casebook

Series 1

EPISODE ONE: **NOTHING BUT THE TRUTH**
TRANSMISSION DATE: **3 JANUARY 1995**
LENGTH: **120 MINS**
WRITER: **RUSSELL LEWIS**
DIRECTOR: **COLIN GREGG**

Kavanagh goes back to his roots, Manchester Crown Court, to defend boxer Clive Gardiner on a charge of grievous bodily harm – to be precise, attacking and stabbing a Mr Parry in a dark car park. The return of the prodigal son ensures the presence in court of Kavanagh's parents, Alf and Marjorie. In the witness box, the confused Parry proves no match for Kavanagh and ends up testifying that he was the one with the knife, not Gardiner. Kavanagh has completely destroyed the prosecution case and the jury waste little time in acquitting Gardiner. The family celebrate Kavanagh's success over lunch where they are joined by his dull brother, Grahame, and pushy sister-in-law, Cynthia.

Back in London, Kavanagh and wife Lizzie attend a riverboat party to celebrate Peter Foxcott becoming Head of Chambers. It is an awkward occasion for them both since the guest list also includes Foxcott's barrister friend, Miles Petersham, with whom Lizzie has recently had an affair. When he catches Petersham sidling up to Lizzie, Kavanagh threatens to kill him if he ever goes near her again. As Petersham slopes off, Lizzie insists that it's all over. Kavanagh wishes he shared her confidence.

The following morning at River Court, Kavanagh is given a brief. 'It's right up your street, sir,' says senior clerk Tom Buckley. 'A nice little rape.'

The 'nice little rape' had allegedly taken place at a large house in Wimbledon where Eve Kendall, a middle-class housewife, had been overseeing the construction of a swimming pool in the garden. The foundations were being laid by builder Gary Porter and David Armstrong, a 21-year-old Cambridge undergraduate earning some pin money during the summer holidays. Armstrong's father is a wealthy industrialist and the son too

GERALDINE JAMES AS ELEANOR HARKER QC.

seems destined for great things in the business world. But Eve Kendall's story, if it proves to be true, stands to bring his blossoming career to a sudden halt.

Her version of events is that one lunch time, after Porter had been called away, she invited Armstrong into the house for a beer and a sandwich. There, she claimed, Armstrong raped her. When her husband returned home in the evening, he found her in a state of hysteria. For his part, Armstrong doesn't deny that he had sex with Mrs Kendall – but claims that she seduced him. With no witnesses, it is her word against his.

EVE KENDALL (ALISON STEADMAN), HAS A SHOCK ENCOUNTER WITH STUDENT DAVID ARMSTRONG.

Armstrong comes across as a personable young man with nothing to hide. Julia Piper, whom Kavanagh would be leading in the defence, is suitably impressed, all the more so since Armstrong's sensible girlfriend Sophie is vowing to stand by him. Julia reasons that no self-respecting girl would cover for a rapist.

Kavanagh's adversary in court is the eminent Eleanor Harker QC but of more concern is the fact that her junior counsel is none other than Miles Petersham. Kavanagh is determined not to let the case degenerate into a personal vendetta between the two men. Harker proceeds to build a formidable case for the prosecution. Eve Kendall is a convincing witness, tearfully reliving her ordeal, and appears to extract a certain amount of sympathy from Judge Granville, a man renowned for his hatred of rapists. If he had his way, they would all hang.

Kavanagh's problems are not confined to court. At the end of the day, he goes for a business meal with Julia, completely forgetting that he is supposed to be at an important fund-raising event organised by Lizzie. By the time he remembers, it is too late. He arrives as the last guests are leaving. Once again, Lizzie concludes that he is putting his work before her.

In his cross-examination of Eve Kendall, Kavanagh shows no mercy, to the despair of his daughter Kate who is watching from the public gallery. His machine-gun delivery soon flusters the witness. Porter and Armstrong had been working on the pool for three weeks yet the only time she asked Armstrong into the house for lunch was when his colleague wasn't there. And all this despite the fact that the defendant brought his own lunch each day in a rucksack. Kavanagh also reveals that Mrs. Kendall had earlier phoned in to the bookshop, where she works part-time, to say that she wouldn't be in that day and, perhaps more crucially, that Mr Kendall was having an affair.

THE TWO FACES OF DAVID ARMSTRONG (RIGHT) THE CASUAL LABOURER (BELOW) THE ANGELIC FACE FOR THE COURTROOM.

The Kendalls had since separated. Kavanagh suggests that Mrs Kendall had sex with David Armstrong to get back at her husband. She weakly denies the allegation but Kavanagh sits down, content that he has done a good job in destroying the witness's credibility. Next, Kavanagh cross- examines the forensic expert about the lack of bruising on Mrs Kendall's body. He forces her to concede that marks on Mrs Kendall's wrists and a bruise on her face are not necessarily consistent with rape. Furthermore, when Alan Kendall, Eve's husband, takes the stand, he confesses that in trying to calm his hysterical wife when he got home that evening, he had grabbed her by the wrists and had slapped her around the face.

By contrast, David Armstrong makes a splendid witness – smartly dressed and scrupulously polite. He stands up well to Harker's relentless questioning. And when she eventually wears him down, making him lose his temper, he responds by delivering an impassioned plea to Eve Kendall. 'Tell them, Eve! Tell them the truth. Why have you done this to me? Eve, please! Why?' The sight of the young man close to tears moves even Kate Kavanagh who had previously been convinced of his guilt.

The jury share Kate's feelings. David Armstrong is found not guilty. As Eve Kendall collapses in tears, the victors go out to celebrate at a nearby wine bar. There Kavanagh is confronted by Clare, a young woman who announces that she was once raped by Armstrong. A stunned Kavanagh is faced with the fact that his triumph has really led to a tragic miscarriage of justice. Returning to his room, he finds his client waiting to thank him. Armstrong extends his hand in gratitude. Kavanagh, disgusted, brushes the gesture aside. Armstrong realises he knows the truth.

Series 1

EPISODE TWO: **HEARTLAND**
TRANSMISSION DATE: **10 JANUARY 1995**
LENGTH: **90 MINS**
WRITER: **RUSSELL LEWIS (based on an idea by Michael Chaplin)**
DIRECTOR: **COLIN GREGG**

On a run-down Sunderland housing estate, former police officer Ray West has organised a group of vigilantes – the Collenshaw Park Pals – to combat crime in the area. One night, while on patrol, he receives a message that there has been a burglary in a nearby street. Shortly afterwards, he spots a local youth, Ryan Jarvis, who has a history of petty crime and whose description matches that of the suspected burglar.

In fact, Jarvis has just left the pub (where his mother works) and has walked West's girlfriend, Lisa Parks, home. When West challenges Jarvis, the teenager taunts him and runs away. West gives chase in his car until Jarvis makes a dash across his path. The ensuing collision leaves Jarvis in a critical condition. He lapses into a coma and is put on a life support machine.

Despite the lack of evidence to the contrary, Jackie Jarvis is convinced that West ran down her son deliberately. She is determined to take out a private prosecution but, since the only witness to the incident is Wrigley, an old man with failing eyesight, Kavanagh strongly advises her to abandon the idea. But when a second witness, Malcolm Gibson, declares himself, she manages to persuade Kavanagh to accept the brief.

RYAN JARVIS LIES IN A COMA FOLLOWING THE INCIDENT WITH THE CAR.

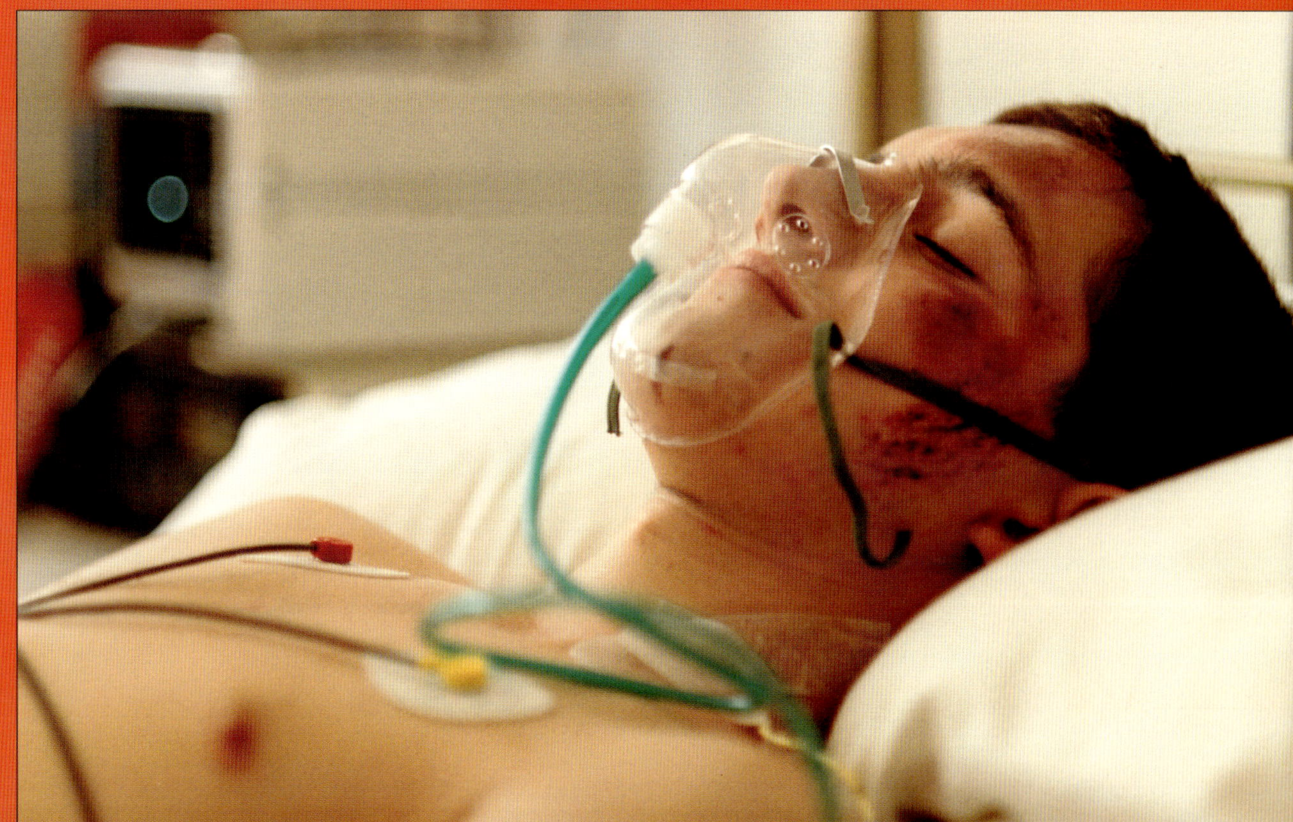

In chambers, Alex Wilson, the black pupil barrister, is sent to represent an obnoxious client in a hopeless case. When she duly fails to persuade the magistrates, the client abuses her and Alex begins to question her suitability for the job. Insisting that he is merely endeavouring to comfort her, Aldermarten caresses her leg in the wine bar, causing her to bolt for safety. While an anxious Aldermarten seeks advice from Foxcott, Alex draws strength from Julia. Ultimately Aldermarten apologises but makes it clear that if Alex wants to prosper, she must take the matter no further. She is then offered a tenancy in chambers, giving her a job for life.

Kavanagh's departure for Sunderland comes at an awkward time for the family. Seemingly unsettled by his parents' absence at critical emotional moments, Matt has been underperforming at school and has been withdrawn from the swimming finals for scribbling unflattering graffiti about his headmaster.

JACKIE JARVIS (PHOEBE NICHOLLS) TAKES ADVICE FROM HER SOLICITOR, NICK CARNFORTH (RICHARD PLATT).

In court, Kavanagh's first key witness, Wrigley, is systematically discredited by West's defence counsel, Clive Pendle. His second, Gibson, suffers the same fate when it emerges that he is an alcoholic with a possible grudge against West. Even the fact that he was beaten up by West's supporters in a bid to prevent his court appearance fails to sustain his credibility. It looks like a lost cause. Kavanagh's only hope is to prove that West is lying when he claims that Don Parks, Lisa's father, was with him in the car when he hit Ryan Jarvis.

Then Kavanagh discovers that Lisa has been visiting Jarvis in hospital and, in a brilliant cross-examination, gets her to admit that Jarvis walked her home on the fateful night. Suddenly, there is the motive for the pursuit of Jarvis – jealousy. But Kavanagh is not finished yet. Tied in knots by the barrage of questions, Lisa finally confesses that her father was not in the car with West, whereupon West's supporters erupt in fury and begin hurling abuse at the weeping girl. The final nail in West's coffin is, ironically, delivered by one of his staunchest allies, Don Parks, who maintains that West did what he had to do in getting rid of a tearaway like Ryan Jarvis. Even though Jarvis had been innocent of the burglary, Parks claims that he had got away with plenty in the past. Now Ray West had appointed himself judge, jury and executioner.

West is found guilty of attempted murder. Vindicated, Jackie Jarvis, who has been told that Ryan can never recover, decides to let her son die .

Series 1

EPISODE THREE: **A FAMILY AFFAIR**
TRANSMISSION DATE: **17 JANUARY 1995**
LENGTH: **90 MINS**
WRITER: **ADRIAN HODGES**
DIRECTOR: **RENNY RYE**

DISTRAUGHT FATHER MICHAEL DUGGAN (GEORGE COSTIGAN) IS LED AWAY.

Michael Duggan, a successful businessman, has been divorced from his wife Samantha for two years. During this period, he has had custody of his 10-year-old son Peter. Now that Samantha has remarried (to Terry Fisher), she has once more been granted custody of her child. Duggan regards this as an injustice and, driven by a desperate desire to be reunited with Peter, kidnaps the boy from school. Three days later, realising that the bid for freedom is hopeless, he gives himself up.

Although he rarely accepts family cases, Kavanagh appears for him in court. Duggan, who has pleaded guilty, is sentenced to eight months in prison. Languishing in jail, Duggan tells his solicitor, Judy Simmons, that he is determined to regain custody of his son. He also alleges that Peter told him he was being abused by his stepfather. In the forthcoming action, Duggan once again wants to be represented by Kavanagh.

Kavanagh has just finished prosecuting in a case where blue movie star Debbie Drake is charged with possession of obscene material intended for publication. She is no stranger to court appearances. Warming to her honesty and wit, even Kavanagh is surprised by the severity of Judge Baxter's sentence - one year in prison. Kavanagh takes no pleasure in this particular victory.

At River Court, Aldermarten's political ambitions take a great leap forward when he is shortlisted for a Conservative Party candidacy. Discovering that his bachelor status is viewed as a shortcoming, he persuades the reluctant Julia to pose as his fiancee. Despite a display of charm and suavity, he sees his hopes crash when the selection committee opt for a car dealer. Politics, Aldermarten reflects, is a dirty business.

TUG-OF-LOVE CHILD PETER GETS A HUG FROM MUM.

When Duggan's case comes to court, the atmosphere is charged with emotion. Duggan's allegation that Peter was abused by his stepfather appears to be without foundation. Social services have found no evidence. Kavanagh concentrates instead on the fact that Peter seems to be a happier, more balanced child when he is living with his natural father than with Terry Fisher. It emerges under cross-examination that, rather than

MICHAEL DUGGAN'S SOLICITOR JUDY SIMMONS (HOLLY AIRD).

IT EMERGES THAT DUGGAN WOULD STOP AT NOTHING TO GAIN CUSTODY OF HIS SON.

bear a second child which might come between her and Fisher, Samantha had an abortion. She also tells the court that Peter told her of the alleged abuse but that, rather than lose Fisher, she kept quiet about it. After much deliberation and a meeting with the boy himself, the judge finds in Duggan's favour and grants him a residence order.

Peter turns up unexpectedly at the court just as the protagonists are leaving and asks his father whether the family can now be reunited, as Duggan had promised. The onlookers listen with horror as it becomes clear that Duggan instructed Peter to lie about the abuse in return for a pledge that Duggan and Samantha would be reconciled. Finally the boy, betrayed by his own father, goes to live with his mother. But Terry Fisher, realising that nothing can ever be the same again, has decided to leave her.

Caught up in this emotional maelstrom, Kavanagh instructs his senior clerk never to involve him in a family case again. At home, Kavanagh's daughter Kate, having secured her father's reluctant permission to allow her boyfriend Luke to stay over, decides not to exercise her option – much to Kavanagh's relief.

Series 1

EPISODE FOUR: **THE SWEETEST THING**
TRANSMISSION DATE: **24 JANUARY 1995**
LENGTH: **90 MINS**
WRITER: **ADRIAN HODGES**
DIRECTOR: **PAUL GREENGRASS**

Celebrating a successful take-over bid, controversial businessman Patrick Hutton visits a West End club with his lieutenant, Randall. As Hutton telephones his wife to say that he is staying the night at a London hotel, he eyes a prostitute, Annie Lewis, sitting at the bar. He invites her back to his hotel where the duty manager, Bobby Day, clearly unhappy at Annie's presence, tries to take Hutton to one side. But the tycoon gives him the brush-off.

Half an hour after Hutton and Annie retire to Hutton's room, Day sees Annie running from the hotel. The following morning, Hutton is found dead in his room, the autopsy suggesting that he was killed between 3am and 4am. His wallet and briefcase are missing. Annie is duly charged with murder.

While Kavanagh acquaints himself with the details of the case, his wife Lizzie is being interviewed for an important fund-raising job in Strasbourg. Although he wishes her luck, Kavanagh is concerned about the effects of prolonged absences on their relationship.

PROSTITUTE ANNIE LEWIS (ANASTASIA HILLE) FACES A CHARGE OF MURDER.

Annie Lewis admits that she was in Hutton's room and that she stole his lighter. But she maintains that she left the hotel at 1am – at least two hours before Hutton was killed. Duty manager Day, however, is adamant that he saw her run out at 3am. Nor are her chances improved by the re-appearance of her former partner, Des Carter, who suddenly produces one of the diaries in which she once recorded her desire to kill men in a particularly savage manner. When Annie refuses to give Carter money, he releases the diaries and provides the Press with photos of Annie. Prosecuting

ONE APPEAL THAT GOES AGAINST KAVANAGH IS AN UNLIKELY LBW DECISION AT THE CHAMBERS CRICKET MATCH.

counsel (Kavanagh's Head of Chambers, Peter Foxcott) can hardly believe his good fortune.

Awaiting trial, Annie is visited by her sister, Diane, and Tracey, Annie's four-year-old daughter whom Diane looks after. She also has two consultations with Kavanagh and Aldermarten, during which it becomes clear that her chances of acquittal are slim. The one other witness who could have testified that she left the hotel at 1am, taxi driver Gerry Hicks, also claims that she didn't get into his cab until 3am.

The annual chambers cricket match against Great Chartham promises a welcome distraction until Foxcott, umpiring, gives an outrageous lbw decision against Kavanagh from which he says there is no appeal. After Kavanagh trudges off bitterly, River Court's day is saved by Julia who, finally persuading Aldermarten to give her a bowl, succeeds in taking the match-winning wicket. She marks her triumph by falling for the opposing captain's chat-up line of 'I've got a complete set of Wisden', and ends up spending the night with him.

In court, Kavanagh is at his most brilliant. In a series of incisive cross-examinations, he succeeds in demonstrating that the taxi driver and the duty manager are unreliable witnesses and that the latter, as Annie has always claimed, has a motive for testifying against her. This is because he provides prostitutes for clients at the hotel but resents Annie because she has steadfastly refused to pay him a cut. Kavanagh also persuades the jury that Annie's youthful diaries were merely the desperate outpourings of a victim cruelly treated by Carter, her erstwhile pimp. Annie is found not guilty.

On the domestic front, Lizzie has accepted the job in Europe with Kavanagh's blessing. Matt is delivered to Lizzie's mother's and Kavanagh boards the Strasbourg flight at Heathrow. He is determined not to neglect Lizzie again.

LOW-LIFE LOTHARIO DES CARTER (JESSE BIRDSALL).

Series 2

EPISODE ONE: **TRUE COMMITMENT**
LENGTH: **90 MINS**
WRITER: **ADRIAN HODGES**
DIRECTOR: **ANDREW GRIEVE**

Miriam Jacobs, daughter of wealthy Jewish businessman Alan Jacobs and recent recruit to an extreme left-wing organisation, plans, with her boyfriend Mark Holland, to embark on the ultimate direct action. On a forthcoming demo, they intend to eliminate a member of the neo-Nazi opposition. Mark appears totally committed to the idea, if only because he is sexually obsessed with Miriam.The demo erupts in violence, and a 17-year-old skinhead, Ian Taylor, is cornered in a garden and stabbed to death in a scuffle. A bloodstained knife lies by the side of his body. Miriam is covered in blood. Mark, who was also involved in the struggle, pockets the knife and makes a run for it but is quickly arrested.

FANATICAL MIRIAM JACOBS (CENTRE) ORCHESTRATES THE LEFT-WING DEMONSTRATION, ENDING IN THE DEATH OF A YOUNG SKINHEAD.

Quizzed at the station by DCI Knowland and DS Vestey, Mark claims that the killing was an accident. He says the knife was Taylor's and that he was pushed on to the victim while he held the knife. But when Miriam is subsequently questioned, she tells a different story. Acting on advice from her father and his solicitor, Michael Hopcraft, she lays the blame squarely on Mark. Stunned by her betrayal, Mark changes his tune and insists that Miriam stabbed Taylor.

In chambers, Aldermarten falls for a woman named Lucy Cartwright, having successfully defended her on a charge of theft. But Aldermarten soon learns to his cost that as far as Lucy is concerned, old habits die hard.

Kavanagh is fighting an uphill battle on two fronts. His home life is rocked by the news that Kate, now a Cambridge undergraduate, is having an affair with her married tutor, Jeffrey Manners, whose wife Angela just happens to be a friend of Lizzie's. And the circumstantial evidence against Mark Holland is overwhelming. Kavanagh's only hope is to cast doubt on Miriam's testimony. And that rests on persuading Kathy Tyler, who lives in the same house as Mark and who was also at the rally, to speak out.

However, there is good news for Kavanagh. Lizzie, frustrated by the bureaucracy of Strasbourg, hands in her notice to her boss, M Kaplan, and, returns home for good.

PROSECUTING COUNSEL DOMINIC BLAKE QC (JOHN WELLS).

Series 2

EPISODE TWO: **MEN OF SUBSTANCE**
LENGTH: **90 MINS**
WRITER: **MATTHEW HALL**
DIRECTOR: **CHARLES BEESON**

RIGHT: SELF-MADE MAN KEVIN GREGSON WITH HIS WIFE AND CHILD.

Endeavouring to stem the tide of drugs from Holland, a team of customs officers led by Simon Lloyd tails a suspicious load of contaminated meat from Harwich to a South London trading estate. The arrival of the load is witnessed by Patrick Bennett, the manager of the depot, and Kevin Gregson, a self-made man with a dubious past. Gregson has aspirations to professional and social respectability but shows little appetite for the conventional methods of achieving them. When the customs team raid the warehouse, the driver, Dieter Klausen, manages to escape but Gregson and Bennett are arrested. Examination of the contaminated carcasses reveal that they contain 15 kilos of heroin.

Initially, customs brief an ageing barrister to prosecute the case but, when he suffers a heart attack, Kavanagh takes his place. Meanwhile Gregson is represented by an extremely bright, ambitious counsel, Susannah Dixon, who relishes the prospect of a head-to-head with Kavanagh and, all too aware that the case will be widely reported, knows what it could do for her career. Dixon declares that her client is prepared to plead guilty to the importation of contaminated meat but denies any knowledge of drugs.

For his part, Bennett is represented by Graham Emerton, an effective though unremarkable barrister, who faces a well nigh impossible task since the circumstantial evidence against his client is formidable. But Gregson's position is less tenuous and Kavanagh knows that he must somehow prove that Gregson knowingly imported the heroin and was not simply present on its arrival. But for Kavanagh, the case comes a little too close to home when Lizzie is followed through London and threatened. It makes him more determined than ever to see that justice is done.

KEVIN GREGSON WITH HIS PARTNER IN CRIME, PATRICK BENNETT.

Meanwhile, River Court's senior clerk, Tom Buckley, whose wife is suffering from a bout of postnatal depression, jeopardises his career in chambers by behaving abrasively at a social gathering for barristers and their wives. On the domestic front, Kavanagh's son Matt has his heart broken by Miranda Lawson, a Sloaney Helen of Troy, who ditches him for a young sprig of the aristocracy, and Lizzie lands a new job as fund-raiser for a large hospital project.

Series 2

EPISODE THREE: **THE BURNING DECK**

LENGTH: **90 MINS**

WRITER: **RUSSELL LEWIS**

DIRECTOR: **CHARLES BEESON**

Lieutenant Ralph Kinross, son of Vice Admiral Kinross, and Marine Engineering Mechanic Patrick Jones are jointly charged with arson and face a court martial in Portsmouth. It is alleged by the prosecutor, Lt Commander Mills, that the crime was a revenge attack against Marine Engineering Mechanic O'Brien.

Mills states that while on a tour of duty aboard HMS Merlin, Jones lent O'Brien the sum of £300. When O'Brien failed to repay the loan, Jones complained to Chief Petty Officer Evans, Falklands veteran and sailor of the old school. Evans suggested that O'Brien pay the money back in instalments. Not satisfied with this, Jones approached Kinross who grew up in the same village as he did.

KAVANAGH OFFERS ELEANOR HARKER A BAG OF CHIPS – ALONG WITH A SYMPATHETIC EAR.

Hearing that Jones had tried to enlist the help of an officer, the rest of the crew began a series of cruel practical jokes with Jones as the prime target. These culminated in his being deliberately locked in the engine room during a fire drill. Suspecting that Evans had turned a blind eye to the bullying, Kinross wrote a highly critical report which, when ratified by his superior, would effectively deny Evans a last chance of promotion and force him to leave the Navy 10 years earlier than he had planned.

However, feeling that Kinross had been compromised by his friendship with Jones, the ship's Captain relieved the officer of his duties. Once the crew reached dry land, it is alleged that Kinross and Jones, using the former's cigarette lighter and a can of lighter fuel, set fire to O'Brien's bunk. Evans claims he saw Kinross leave the accommodation block immediately after fire broke out.

While Foxcott is being pestered by the Dromgooles, a pair of campaigning Christians, who run the National Council for the Conservation of Moral Standards, Kavanagh sets out to represent Kinross at the court martial. Acting for Jones is Kavanagh's old friend and foe, Eleanor Harker QC, for whom the trial proves a particularly uncomfortable experience since her husband has just left her. Kavanagh is similarly ill at ease. The deeper he delves into the case, the more puzzling it becomes. But that could be because his client is withholding a vital piece of information...

Series 2

EPISODE FOUR: **A SENSE OF LOSS**
LENGTH: **90 MINS**
WRITER: **MATTHEW HALL**
DIRECTOR: **CHARLES BEESON**

A young policewoman, Clare Kemble , is murdered while investigating a robbery at a newsagents. The police arrest Paul Warwick, a youth with a long history of petty theft. Paul acts as surrogate father to his younger brother Terry who sustained brain damage some years earlier as a result of joyriding with Paul. The evidence against Paul is damning. A witness saw him running away from the scene and an identical gun to the murder weapon was found in his room together with a training shoe bearing traces of Clare's blood. Worst of all, Paul has made a full confession to the police and refuses to help his defence counsel, Kavanagh. However, Kavanagh suspects there is more to the case than meets the eye.

Series 2

EPISODE FIVE: **A STRANGER IN THE FAMILY**
LENGTH: **90 MINS**
WRITER: **PAUL HINES**
DIRECTOR: **ANDREW GRIEVE**

David Lomax, a brilliant young marine engineering student, is working during his vacation at the East Bankside Recycling Centre on the Thames. For some time, the centre has been treating medical waste in an irresponsible fashion, simply bagging it and throwing it into containers. One day, noticing an open container on the barge, David draws it to the attention of the foreman, Pearson.

At that moment, the site manager, Dale, whose paramount interest is the bottom line, arrives and orders David on to the barge. Pearson, distracted by the need to discuss lax methods with Dale, switches off the main power but, after an argument with his boss, turns it back on again while David is still aboard. As a result, David is struck by a swinging container and falls into the hold, sustaining spinal and brain damage. Baxter, a disaffected young colleague who operates the crane, denies all knowledge of the accident.

Facing a lifetime of care, David's parents, Sam and Gina, are determined to make a claim against the recycling centre. Their solicitor, Martin Haslam, takes the case to River Court where Julia Piper chooses Kavanagh as her leader, even though he has not done a personal injury case for 20 years.

While Aldermarten applies for 'silk' and visits the tailors where a silver-tongued assistant talks him into spending money, Kavanagh meets up again with Helen Ames, a gifted barrister from a working-class background, with whom he first crossed swords some years earlier. She abandoned the Law while having her baby but now, hearing that Julia is about to leave River Court, is eager to resume her career.

Besieged at home by Matt who is conducting a campaign for a car, Kavanagh escapes to visit a treatment centre in an attempt to understand fully David Lomax's condition. The hard-pressed consultant, Diana Walsh, makes it clear that David will be a burden on his family until he dies.

When the Lomax case comes to court before Judge Swarbrick, Diana Walsh and the defence consultant, Marsh, give conflicting evidence as to David's capabilities. Crosby, the experienced defence counsel, endeavours to demonstrate that David is not as disabled as he would have people believe. But Kavanagh is determined to see that justice is done and sets out to break the three defence witnesses, Baxter, Dale and Pearson.

Series 2

EPISODE SIX: **JOB SATISFACTION**
LENGTH: **90 MINS**
WRITER: **ADRIAN HODGES**
DIRECTOR: **COLIN GREGG**

When David and Alice Pembridge are found dead at their farm with shotgun wounds, David's children by his first marriage, Sam and Caroline, are charged with their murder. Sam elects to defend himself while Kavanagh represents Caroline. In court, the defendant's half-brother , Duncan Pembridge, reveals that a month before the murders, David had refused to lend Sam money to set up a publishing company. Sam counters by pointing out that, if he and Caroline are convicted, Duncan would become sole beneficiary. Is Duncan manufacturing the evidence to suit his own ends? Meanwhile Kavanagh has to come to terms with a personal tragedy.

APPENDIX

Cast lists

REGULAR CAST

JAMES KAVANAGH Q.C. .... **John Thaw**
LIZZIE KAVANAGH.......... **Lisa Harrow**
JULIA PIPER.......... **Anna Chancellor**
PETER FOXCOT .... **Oliver Ford Davies**
JEREMY ALDERMARTEN ..... **Nicholas Jones**
TOM BUCKLEY .... **Cliff Parisi**
ALEX WILSON............. **Jenny Jules**
KATE KAVANAGH............ **Daisy Bates**
MATT KAVANAGH........... **Tom Brodie**

PRINCIPLE GUEST ARTISTS

(In alphabetical order)

SERIES ONE

Nothing But The Truth

LORD PROBYN.................. *Robin Bailey*
CYNTHIA KAVANAGH........... *Rosalind Bailey*
MRS GREAVES................ *Joan Blackham*
PROFESSOR BELLAMY........... *Philip Bowen*
PARRY...................... *John Brobbey*
ALAN KENDALL.................. *David Cardy*
GARY PORTER............. *Danny Cunningham*
SOPHIE..................... *Elli Garnett*
CLARE...................... *Juliette Gruber*
JOCK ARMSTRONG............... *Terence Harvey*
MARJORIE KAVANAGH............ *Jean Heywood*
MR GREAVES.............. *Maxwell Hutcheon*
ELEANOR HARKER QC .... *Geraldine James*
ALFRED KAVANAGH............ *George Malpas*
DAVID ARMSTRONG........... *Ewan McGregor*
LUKE........................ *Nick Patrick*
FIONA MARSHALL.............. *Ruth Redman*
JUDGE GRANVILLE.............. *Paul Rogers*
EVE KENDALL............... *Alison Steadman*
MILES PETERSHAM............... *Pip Torrens*
GRAHAME KAVANAGH........... *Albert Welling*
CLIVE GARDINER............... *Oliver Wilson*

Heartland

DON PARKS..................... *Mike Elliott*
KEITH....................... *Alan Gilchrist*
SHERYL REBEKAH................. *Joy Gilgan*
CLIVE PENDLE.............. *Robert Glenister*
RAY WEST.................. *Richard Graham*
STAN WRIGLEY................ *Harry Herring*
JUDGE GARTON................. *John Horsley*
DR. ELLEN ATKINS................. *Judi Lamb*
LISA MARIE PARKS........... *Angela Lonsdale*
JACKIE JARVIS............... *Phoebe Nicholls*
NICK CARNFORTH.............. *Richard Platt*
MALCOLM GIBSON............... *Ralph Riach*
RYAN JARVIS................. *Shaun Roberts*

A Family Affair

JUDY SIMMONS.................... *Holly Aird*
DI BRYCE..................... *Robert Ashby*
MICHAEL BARNARD......... *Michael Bertenshaw*
JUDGE FAIRFAX................ *Adrian Cairns*
MICHAEL DUGGAN........... *George Costigan*
ROY HESTON.................. *Richard Dixon*
PATRICIA RUNCORN............ *Shirley Dixon*
GEOFF GREEN................. *Mike Dowling*
PETER DUGGAN................ *Peter England*
ELAINE WINSTON................ *Annie Hayes*
SAMANTHA FISHER............. *Phyllis Logan*
HELEN WILKES.............. *Kate Lynn-Evans*
HILARY DIXON............... *Myra McFadyen*
LUKE........................ *Nick Patrick*
HEADMASTER................. *Neville Phillips*

Terry Fisher .... *Dougray Scott*
Judge Baxter .... *Tim Seely*
Justice Griffin .... *John Shrapnel*
Deborah Drake .... *Toyah Willcox*
Nayana Singh .... *Rita Wolf*

The Sweetest Thing

Des Carter .... *Jesse Birdsall*
Bobby Day .... *Stephen Boxer*
Judge Trafford .... *John Carlisle*
Dr Derek Buxton .... *Sam Cox*
Diane .... *Ellie Haddington*
Susan Hutton .... *Carol Harrison*
Sir David Taylor .... *John Hart Dyke*
Patrick Hutton .... *Tony Haygarth*
Dr Jeffrey Markham .... *Colin Higgins*
Annie Lewis .... *Anastasia Hille*
Tony Hayes .... *Edward Holmes*
Kaplan .... *Peter Hudson*
David Lurie .... *William Masson*
Lady Anne Probyn .... *Mary Miller*
Gerry Hicks .... *Robert Oates*
Luke .... *Nick Patrick*
Dave Randall .... *Mark Strong*
DI Wilton .... *Gary Whelan*

SERIES TWO

True Commitment

Kathy Tyler .... *Harriet Ashcroft*
Angela Manners .... *Selina Cadell*
Alan Jacobs .... *Nicholas Day*
Jeffrey Manners .... *Rob Edwards*
Prof Michael Hart .... *Peter Harlowe*
Dr. Alan Morley .... *Michael Haughey*
Kaplan .... *Peter Hudson*
Patricia Graves .... *Lucy Jenkins*
Mark Holland .... *Stuart Laing*
Lucy Cartwright .... *Lesley Manville*
Ian Taylor .... *Scott Mitchell*
Nick Stevens .... *Michael Rogerson*
Miriam Jacobs .... *Doraly Rosen*
Marcia Jacobs .... *Carmen Du Sautoy*
Griffiths .... *Charles Simpson*
Judge Tremain .... *Michael Stroud*
Dominic Blake QC .... *John Wells*
DCI Knowland .... *Michael Williams*

Men of Substance

Graham Emerton .... *Dermot Crowley*
Alan Pearson .... *Ken Drury*
Chris Starkey .... *Martyn Ellis*
Jenny Norris .... *Ruth Gemmell*
Judge Phipson .... *James Greene*
Susannah Dixon .... *Clare Higgins*
Dieter Klausen .... *Wolf Kahler*
Simon Lloyd .... *John McArdle*
David Maddox .... *Robert Murray*
Kevin Gregson .... *Jonathan Phillips*
Eleanor Foxcott .... *Celestine Randall*
Mandy Gregson .... *Kit Scanlon Jones*
Charles Fordham .... *Mark Searle*
Miranda .... *Amy Simcock*
Patrick Bennett .... *Stephen Tate*
Sarah Lee Gordon .... *Tamara Ustinov*
Dr Webber .... *James Warrior*

The Burning Deck

Burrell .... *Richard Bacon*
Cynthia Kavanagh .... *Rosalind Bailey*
Captain Ian Tredinnick .... *Keith Bartlett*
Lt Commander Hugh Mills .... *Sean Chapman*
Commander Driscoll .... *William Chubb*
Mrs Dromgoole .... *Jane Freeman*
MEM Patrick Jones .... *Alan Gilchrist*
Eleanor Harker QC .... *Geraldine James*
Helen Kinross .... *Tamzin Malleson*
Harris .... *David Mallinson*
Vice Admiral Kinross .... *Hugh Millais*
Lt Ralph Kinross .... *Rupert Penry-Jones*
Mrs Jones .... *Pamela Ruddock*

David LurieWilliam . . . . *Scott Masson*
MEM O'Brien . . . . *Andy Serkis*
Noel Dromgoole . . . . *James Taylor*
Grahame Kavanagh . . . . *Albert Welling*
CPO Evans . . . . *Ray Winstone*

A Sense of Loss

Lord Probyn .Robin Bailey
DC Rook .James Barriscale
WPC Clare Kemble . . . . .Selina Boyack
Paul Warwick . . . . .Ruaidhri Conroy
Oyinda Barruba . . . . .Anni Domingo
Mr Justice Danforth . . . . .Donald Douglas
DS Richards .Karl Draper
Roger Cooper . . . . .Roger Frost
Scarsdale . . . . .Robin Hooper
PC Wooller . . . . .Gerald Horan
DI Washbrook . . . . .Grant Masters
Terry Warwick . . . . .Iain Robertson
Martin Redcar . . . . .Martin Ronan
Brian Yeats . . . . .Willie Ross
Maggie Warwick . . . . .Ger Ryan
Damon Marshall . . . . .Chris Sonning
Claudia . . . . .Sylvia Syms

A Stranger in the family

Diana Walsh . . . .*Janet Amsbury*
Shop assistant . . . . *Robert Ashby*
Usher . . . . *Tim Barron*
Gosling . . . . *Timothy Bentinck*
Anne Pearson . . . . *Eileen Davies*
Dr Gupta . . . . *Norma Dixit*
Pearson . . . . *Alfred Lynch*
Baxter . . . . *Stephen Marcus*
Sam Lomax . . . . *Colin McCormack*
Crosby . . . . *T P McKenna*
David Lomax . . . . *Kevin McKidd*
Therapist . . . . *Sian Radinger*
Marsh . . . . *Peter Reeves*
Martin Haslam . . . . *David Schneider*
Judge Swarbrick . . . . *Ned Sherrin*
Gina Lomax . . . . *Frances Tomelty*
Dale . . . . *John Wheatley*
Helen Ames . . . . *Arkie Whiteley*

Job Satisfaction

Cynthia Kavanagh . . . . *Rosalind Bailey*
Female Prison Warder . . . . *Jelena Budimir*
Judge Ransome . . . . *Michael Byne*
Clerk of the Court . . . . *Nigel Carrington*
Duncan Pembridge . . . . *Robert Cavanah*
Barbara Tully . . . . *Marty Cruickshank*
Staff Nurse . . . . *Karen Davies*
Caroline Wicks . . . . *Emma Fielding*
Policeman . . . . *Grahame Fox*
Marjorie Kavanagh . . . . *Jean Heywood*
Lord Justice Fenwick . . . . *Richard Johnson*
Gerry Wainwright . . . . *Bob Kingdom*
Ashol Prasad QC . . . . *Art Malik*
Alfred Kavanagh . . . . *George Malpas*
Reporter . . . . *Harry Nicholls*
Connor . . . . *Aron Paramor*
Sam Wicks . . . . *Paul Rhys*
Diana Taylor . . . . *Vivienne Ritchie*
Dr Michael Ashurst . . . . *David Terence*
Grahame Kavanagh . . . . *Albert Welling*
Helen Ames . . . . *Arkie Whiteley*

PRODUCTION TEAM

Executive producer . . . . *Ted Childs*
Producer . . . . *Chris Kelly*
Associate producer . . . . *Lars Macfarlane*
Directors (Series Two) . . . . *Charles Beeson*
. . . . *Andrew Grieve*
. . . . *Colin Gregg*
Designer . . . . *Michael Pickwood*
Director of photography . . . . . . *Nigel Walters*
Production coordinator . . . . *Liz Watkins*
Costume designer . . . . *Sue Yelland*

Wardrobe supervisor . . . . *Tony Allen*
Asst. Wardrobe supervisor . . . . . *Lindsay Pugh*
Make-up supervisor . . . . *Sarah Grundy*
Make-up artists . . . . *Nicola Perkins*
. . . . *Margaret O'Keefe*
Location manager . . . . *David Kennaway*
Asst location manager . . . . *Pat Karam*
Location assistant . . . . *Tillie Williams*
Producer's assistant . . . . *Sarah Manning*
Production runner . . . . *Alexandra Eastman*
1st assistant directors . . . . *Sam Harris*
. . . . *Martin Harrison*
2nd assistant director . . . . *Sarah Dibsdall*
3rd assistant director . . . . *Sean Clayton*
Script editor . . . . *Rob Pursey*
Script supervisors . . . . *Lorely Farley*
. . . . *Pauline Harlow*
Casting director . . . . *Joyce Gallie*
Casting co-ordinator . . . . *Sally Osoba*
Camera operators . . . . *Rodrigo Gutierrez*
. . . . *Noel Probyn*
Focus pullers . . . . *Nick Lowin*
. . . . *Martin Shepherd*
Clapper loader . . . . *Harriet Carpenter*
Grip . . . . *Alfie Williams*
Sound mixer . . . . *Ian Voigt*
Sound maintenance engineer . . . *Steve O'Brien*
Art director . . . . *Henry Harris*
Asst. art director . . . . *Katie Buckley*
Art dept. asst. . . . . *Miranda Cull*
Production buyer . . . . *Jeanne Vertigan*
Asst. production buyer . . . . *Jo Barrs*
Property master . . . . *Terry Tague*
Property store keeper . . . . *Jo Tague*
Dressing prop . . . . *Mario Bueno*
Standby props . . . . *Chris Browning*
. . . . *Roger Edwards*
Standby prop driver . . . . *Jim Ryan*
Standby carpenter . . . . *Nigel Crafts*
Standby painter . . . . *Bob Starrett*
Standby rigger . . . . *Andy Moore*
Gaffer . . . . *Alan Muhley*
Best boy . . . . *Ken Sykes*
Electricians . . . . *Gary Chaisty*
. . . . *Dave Oldroyd*
Generator operator . . . . *Tommy Broadhurst*
Editors . . . . *Dave Blackmore*
. . . . *Roger Wilson*
Asst. film editor . . . . *Tracey Jury*
Sound editor . . . . *Simon Gershon*
Post-production supervisors . . . *Shelley Powell*
. . . . *Liz Pearson*
Editing dept. runner . . . . *Robin Holland*
Composer . . . . *John Keane*
Production accountant . . . . *Richard Hyland*
Asst. prod. accountant . . . . *Stella Hyland*
Unit drivers . . . . *Micky Grover*
. . . . *Peter Kyriacou*
. . . . *Barry Newell*
. . . . *Chris Streeter*
Minibus driver . . . . *Melvin Kiernan*
Site supervisor . . . . *Mick Skivington*
Stills photographer . . . . *Tony Nutley*
Utility standins . . . . *Barry Summerford*
. . . . *Julie Brown*
Caterers . . . . *Anglia Catering*

ACKNOWLEDGEMENTS

The author would like to thank the following for their friendly cooperation in the preparation of this book:

Ted Childs, Chris Kelly, John Thaw, Lisa Harrow, Anna Chancellor, Oliver Ford Davies, Nicholas Jones, Cliff Parisi, Daisy Bates, Tom Brodie, Charles Beeson, David Bradly, Michael Pickwoad, Lars Macfarlane, Joyce Gallie, Sue Yelland, Sarah Grundy, Margaret O'Keefe, Nigel Walters, Sarah Manning, Roger Wilson, David Kennaway, Pat Karam, Russell Lewis, Matthew Hall, Jeanne Vertigan, Jo Barrs, Deborah Waight, Fiona Connery, Nick Lockett, Barry Ledingham and, from Carlton Books, Lorraine Dickey.